PEACE AND NON-VIOLENCE

edited by
EDWARD GUINAN

PEACE and NONVIOLENCE

basic writings

PAULIST PRESS
New York   Paramus   Toronto

Library of Congress
Catalog Card Number: 73-75741

ISBN: 0-8091-1770-3

Published by Paulist Press
Editorial Office: 1865 Broadway, N.Y., N.Y. 10023
Business Office: 400 Sette Drive, Paramus, N.J. 07652

Printed and bound in the
United States of America

ACKNOWLEDGMENTS

We are grateful to the following publishers and individuals for permission to reprint copyrighted material (those articles not listed are in the public domain):

Bergman Publishers for "Reply to Critics," from *On Civil Disobedience and Non-Violence* by Leo Tolstoy (1967).

Daniel Berrigan for "A Meditation from Catonsville."

The Bobbs-Merrill Company, Inc. for "Declaration of Sentiments, 1838," by William Lloyd Garrison, and for "First Letter to the Delaware Indians," by William Penn, from *Non-Violence in America: A Documentary History,* Staughton Lynd, editor (1965).

The Catholic Worker for "Fall Appeal" (October-November, 1971), "Catholic Worker Positions" (May, 1972) and "Not the Smallest Grain of Incense," by Tom Cornell.

Danilo Dolci for "Excerpt from Newsletters," from *Outlaws.* English translation by R. Munroe is used by permission of Grossman Publishers. Copyright © 1961 by The Orion Press, Inc.

The Estate of Martin Luther King, Jr. for "Suffering and Faith," copyright © 1960. Reprinted by permission of Joan Daves.

Fellowship magazine for "Love in Action," by Thich Nhat Hanh (January 1970) and "Christ's Teachings," by Vinoba Bhave (May 1960).

Fellowship Publications for "The Workability of Non-Violence," by A. J. Muste.

Hildegaard Goss-Mayr for "Active Non-Violence."

Thich Nhat Hanh for "Condemnation."

A special acknowledgment and thanks to Rachelle Linner as special research and editing assistant, Mary Caron, Dave Green, Rich Marold, Cherie Loustaunau and Lorraine Yenulevich for manuscript work, and Rev. Jack Wintermyer for making his books available. More important than the product that resulted was their friendship, community and enthusiasm for peace, which nourished us all through the long months of work.

Contents

viii   *Contents*

Dedicated to a new generation of resisters
who accept neither plunder nor clichés

"Do you know, Fontanes, what astonishes me most in this world? The inability of force to create anything. In the long run the sword is always beaten by the spirit."

Napoleon

The awareness of a universal brotherhood is developing in our world, at least in principle. Whoever works to educate the rising generations in the conviction that every man is our brother is building from the foundation the edifice of peace. Whoever implants in public opinion the sentiment of human brotherhood, without any limits, is preparing better days for the world. Whoever conceives of the protection of political interests as a logical and organic necessity of social life, without the incitement of hate and combat among men, is opening to human society the ever effective advancement of the common good. Whoever helps in discovering in every man— beyond his physical, ethical, ethnic and racial characteristics—the existence of a being equal to his own, is transforming the earth from an epicenter of division, antagonism, treachery and revenge into a field of vital work for civil collaboration. *For where brotherhood among men is at root disregarded, peace is at root destroyed.* And yet peace is the mirror of real, authentic, modern humanity, victorious over every anachronistic self-injury. Peace is the great concept extolling love among men, who discover that they are brothers and decide to live as such.

Paul VI

If We Listen Well

For too long we have considered peace as the absence of conflict. We have approached the issue with this limited perspective and have directed our attention to the prevailing conflict of the moment, attempting to discover ways of reducing the destructiveness of the event. This approach is both necessary and desirable, but insufficient as we continue to approach the problem in a fragmented and isolated way. We continue to deal in symptomatic terms as war and destruction and violence are the extensions and natural outgrowths of malignant attitudes, values, relationships and beliefs that we continue to embrace.

Peace

Conflict will always be an integral part of human life but our methods of dealing with it need to change. We must be willing to develop an ongoing critical view of our values, operating premises and relationships, and a sensitivity to those about us.

Peace demands that one anticipate the effects of his views and actions on others and the unifying or destructive effects they may have. Most importantly one comes to realize that the "end" does not justify the "means": we get what we do, not what we hope for or intend. You cannot improve a man through punishment, nor can you bring peace through war or brotherhood through brutalization.

Finally one comes to apppreciate the reality that there can be no "we's" and "they's" in our lives, but only brothers and sisters—all children of God—all sacred and dignified. Destruction of any one of these God-gifts means a certain destruction of oneself, and a mystery that is gone forever from this small, fragile world.

Violence

Violence can be seen as destructive communication. Any adequate definition must include physical, verbal, symbolic, psycho-

1

logical and spiritual displays of hostility and hatred. The definition must include both our acts and our inactions and that which is done directly to people or indirectly to them through what they esteem. Many forms will take on a combination of these characteristics.

Violence should then include physical acts against another (i.e., the range of acts from personal attack to war, that which violates human autonomy and integrity); verbal attacks that demean and humiliate; symbolic acts that evoke fear and hostility; psychological attitudes that deny one's humanity and equality (legal, institutional and moral); spiritual postures that communicate racism, inferiority and worthlessness (i.e., beliefs and values that demean or categorize). Violence then becomes a dynamic rather than merely an act.

Hunger, poverty, squalor, privilege, powerlessness, riches, despair, and vicarious living are forms of violence—forms that a society approves and perpetuates. We have been too willing to discuss violence in terms of ghetto uprisings, student unrest, street thievery and trashing, and have been unwilling to direct our attention to the more pathological types of violence that are acceptable—the types that daily crush the humanity and life from untold millions of brothers and sisters.

In the sixties we spoke with alarm of the "increase of violence" in our society, which may be a half-truth: violence became more democratic in the decade of the sixties. Instead of resting exclusively with those who construct and maintain ghettos, keep food from the mouths of children and coerce the young through educational programming and into war, violence became the tool of a widely divergent group seeking equality, power and redress.

Under the umbrella of violence there reside two distinctively different phenomena. First there is the violence of men and women who act out of frustration, hopelessness and anger in an attempted grasp at life—the act of the slave breaking the chains, which is understandable and inevitable as long as some humans are in bondage. The other type of violence is the violence of the respectable, the violence of the powerful that seeks personal gain and privilege by maintaining inhuman conditions. It is the violence of the board rooms, legislators and jurists—the white collar violence that pours surplus milk down sewers, robs workers of their wages, maintains prisons of infamy, lies to children, discards the weak and old and insists that some should half-live while others rape and ravage the earth. This latter type of violence is what we must become aware of and actively dismantle if the future is to hold any possibilities for peace and a world where all men and women have a right to live and develop and participate by reason of their humanity, not by reason of their class, productive ability or shrewdness.

Non-Violence

Non-violence cannot then be understood as passivity or indifference to the dynamic of life (i.e., communication between men). It is not the posture of removing oneself from conflict that marks the true non-violent man, but, quite on the contrary, it is placing oneself at the heart of that dynamic. Non-violence means taking the responsibility for aiding the direction of human communication and brotherhood. Non-violence means an active opposition to those acts and attitudes that demean and brutalize another, and it means an active support of those values and expressions that foster human solidarity. Non-violence, in essence, means taking a stand in favor of life and refusing to delegate individual moral responsibility to another person or group; it means taking control of one's life and aiding others in doing likewise. Non-violence is an attempt to find truth and love even in the midst of hatred, destruction and pride.

As the means cannot be separated from the desired ends, non-violence cannot be separated from peace, for it is the value system and dynamic that makes peace possible.

The text has a twofold purpose. It is a resource book not meant to be used as a text where one proceeds from one chapter to the next, but a rich combination of materials placed at the disposal of the group for consideration and use. The text includes a wide range of essays, letters, talks, court statements and poems centering on the broad issue of human conflict. Secondly, and most importantly, it is a collection of material and individual religious expressions that challenged the prevailing "values" of the day, either historical or contemporary, by persons capable of standing with their convictions for the enrichment of all. Those listed within these pages are not insignificant men and women, nor should their voices and sacrifices be absent from the educational experience.

The Times

The past has not been given to us; it is not ours to breathe or exhale. We live within the smallest perimeter, which we call today, and into this brief moment, into this small space we beckon and command the future.

These are not good times, but good times do not mold great people. The sins of our excesses and arrogance can destroy us, or these failings can humble us to sainthood. Such are the times.

If the great virtues and teachings of the martyrs, resisters and saints are relegated to a utopian or future-oriented condition, then, indeed, they have little value for us at all. But the great heritage that this "community of liberation" has left us is not some unreal, impossible dream. It is this: Love can, and must, be lived today, despite the pain and difficulty of such life. Tomorrow will carry the tenderness and peace which we live now. Do not compromise today. It is all, dear brothers and sisters, that we have.

The Themes and People

The first signs of a violent society appear in its basic inability to communicate. Words lose their meaning and become hollow. They are twisted and deformed as tools of manipulation and servitude. Noble words such as truth, goodness and love may come to mean despotism, obedience and death. Peace becomes another name for multi-headed war missles, and non-violence is wrenched to mean silence, or lack of opposition, to thievery, privilege and the status quo.

The people who fill these pages are poets, dreamers and priests. They use these words much differently from the way they are commonly heard or understood. They don't use words lightly, nor do they dismiss them without reflection. This assembled community of peacemakers have paid dearly for their belief in such words, and their lives form a chronicle of inspiration. They have been demeaned and laughed at; they have been dragged through jails and courtrooms and prisons; a few have paid the price of peace with their lives.

The editor of this volume finds it unnecessary to argue their case, but merely requests that you read thoughtfully; you may discover that there is a difference between rhetoric and prayer. The former may well impress you, but only the latter will bring you salvation.

The Spiritual

A line from a contemporary song pleads: "Help me make it through the night." We find our existence framed in terms of aloneness rather than solidarity, struggles rather than consummations, departures rather than arrivals, questions rather than answers, and, most importantly, night rather than daylight.

We cry out for fear the night will absorb us, yet we are unsure of any presence; we sing so as not to be crushed, yet the tones reflect the endless chant of the nightingales; we dance so as not to fall prey to these awesome interludes of emptiness; and most of all we pray so as not to lie. And these are the words we might use: "Help us make it through the night."

Yet in the aloneness and struggle, in the departures and questions, in the cries and songs, in the dance and prayers there are imprints of heroic men and women, there are weavings of beauty, there are caresses of God. Traced through the faces of the old are messages of dignity and tenderness. The wail of the newborn is proof of silent breaths conspiring together. Each "forgive me" and "I love you" is prefaced by the warm tides of grace. Saints are born in Harlem in precise rhythm. Young people hurdle concrete mazes to touch and remember. Children weep for lost birds. Monks and mystics pray the sun up in the morning and call the evening dew. There are still wonderment, wishes and dreams.

You must never forget that you are the brother or the sister of a carpenter and the child of a king. You must remember that all life is unfulfilled without you. You may learn that life is mysterious and sacred and that you must never, never destroy it. And if you listen well you will hear the chanting of others, and they are singing to you: "Help us make it through the night."

Edward Guinan, C.S.P.

1 Adin Ballou

Adin Ballou, the founder of the Utopian Hopedale Community in 1841, was also co-founder (with William Lloyd Garrison) and president of the New England Non-Resistance Society. The selections here * are a clear and forceful statement on non-resistance in Gospel terms. As a thinker, Ballou's writings influenced the thought of Thoreau, Tolstoy and Gandhi.

Christian Non-Resistance

Whence originated the term Christian non-resistance? Non-resistance comes from the injunction, "resist not evil," Matt. 5:39. The words "resist not," being changed from the form of a verb to that of a substantive, give us non-resistance. This term is considered more strikingly significant than any other of the principles involved, and the duty enjoined in our Savior's precept. Hence its adoption and established use. It is denominated Christian non-resistance, to distinguish it, as the genuine primitive doctrine, from mere philosophical, sentimental and necessitous non-resistance. Literally, then, Christian non-resistance is the original non-resistance taught and exemplified by Jesus Christ, the bearings, limitations and applications of which are to be learned from the Scriptures of the New Testament.

And what are those bearings, limitations and applications? I

* Reprinted from *Christian Non-Resistance* (Philadelphia: Universal Peace Union, 1910).

7

have already given an imperfect view of them in the previous definitions. But I will be more explicit. What I aim at is to carry the obligations of non-resistance just as far and no farther than Jesus Christ has done. It is easy to go beyond, or to fall short of his limits. Ultra-radicals go beyond him. Ultra-conservatives fall short of him. Even those of both these classes, who profess to abide implicitly by his teachings, construe and interpret his language so as to favor their respective errors. The ultra-radicals seize on strong figurative, hyperbolic, or intensive forms of expression, and make him seem to mean much more than he could have intended. The ultra-conservatives ingeniously fritter away and nullify the very essence of his precepts, in such a manner as to make him seem to mean much less than he must have intended. There is, however, a general rule for such cases, which can scarcely fail to expose the errors of both classes, in respect to any given text. It is this: "Consider the context; consider parallel texts; consider examples; consider the known spirit of Christianity." Any construction or interpretation of the recorded language of Christ, or of his apostles, in which all these concur, is sound. Any other is probably erroneous.

What a Christian Non-Resistant Cannot Consistently Do

It will appear from the foregoing exposition that a true Christian non-resistant cannot, with deliberate intent, knowledge or conscious voluntariness, compromise his principles by either of the following acts.

1. He cannot kill, maim or otherwise absolutely injure any human being, in personal self-defense, or for the sake of his family, or any thing he holds dear.

2. He cannot participate in any lawless conspiracy, mob, riotous assembly, or disorderly combination of individuals, to cause or

countenance the commission of any such absolute personal injury.

3. He cannot be a member of any voluntary association, however orderly, respectable or allowable by law and general consent, which declaratively holds as fundamental truth, or claims as an essential right, or distinctly inculcates as sound doctrine, or approves as commendable in practice, war, capital punishment, or any other absolute personal injury.

4. He cannot be an officer or private, chaplain or retainer, in the army, navy or militia of any nation, state, or chieftain.

5. He cannot be an officer, elector, agent, legal prosecutor, passive constituent, or approver of any government, as a sworn or otherwise pledged supporter thereof, whose civil constitution and fundamental laws require, authorize or tolerate war, slavery, capital punishment, or the infliction of any absolute personal injury.

6. He cannot be a member of any chartered corporation or body politic, whose articles of compact oblige or authorize its official functionaries to resort for compulsory aid in the conducting of its affairs to a government of constitutional violence.

7. Finally, he cannot do any act, either in person or by proxy; nor abet or encourage any act in others; nor demand, petition for, request, advise or approve the doing of any act, by an individual, association or government, which act would inflict, threaten to inflict, or necessarily cause to be inflicted any absolute personal injury, as herein before defined.

Such are the necessary bearings, limitations and applications of the doctrine of Christian non-resistance. Let the reader be careful not to misunderstand the positions laid down. The platform of principle and action has been carefully founded, and its essential peculiarities plainly delineated. Let it not be said that the doctrine goes against all religion, government, social organization, constitutions, laws, order, rules, and regulations. It goes against none of these things *per se*. It goes for them in the highest and best sense. It goes only against such religion, government, social organization, constitutions, laws, order, rules, regulations and restraints as are unequivocally contrary to the law of Christ, as are sanction for taking "life for life, eye for eye, tooth for tooth," as are based on the assumption that it is right to resist injury with injury, evil with evil.

PEACE AND NON-VIOLENCE

OTHER WORKS BY ADIN BALLOU

Autobiography of Adin Ballou, 1803-1890 (Lowell, Mass.: Vox Populi Press, 1896).

Non-Resistance in Relation to Human Governments (Boston: Boston Non-Resistance Society, 1839).

Practical Christian Socialism (New York: Fowlers and Wells, 1854).

2 *Daniel Berrigan, S.J.*

Father Daniel Berrigan is one of the most passionate and articulate members of the growing Catholic radical movement. His actions have been disturbing to many people; what he says is painful to hear. Daniel Berrigan is a poet, a priest, a felon.

The first selection is a letter written by Father Berrigan and smuggled out of the federal prison in Danbury, Conn., where he was incarcerated. The statement was made on the occasion of the end of a fast by war resisters transferred from Danbury to a prison in Springfield, Mo. The second selection is a meditation by Father Berrigan written before he and eight other men and women destroyed draft records in Catonsville, Maryland in May 1968.

A Letter from Jail

Today we celebrate together with 11 men, friends and brothers, an event of some import. Eleven prisoners, friends, brothers, today are sitting down to their first meal in over a month. The celebration, the event, the men involved—all are instructive.

The 11 prisoners, first of all, are worthy of note for a most peculiar reason. They have an unrehabilitated habit of getting themselves into trouble. One month ago they started a fast in Danbury prison, distributed leaflets saying why, and got thrown into solitary. When they persisted and others joined them, the 11 were snatched out of Danbury and flown across country under heavy armaments. It was almost as though they were named Tom Paine or Paul Revere, caught in the act of distributing the Declaration of Independence.

11

It was that absurd. The leaflet that launched a thousand marshals advocated nothing like the overthrow of George III, Thieu, Hoover or any other peerless benefactor of our race. The leaflet merely called attention to the duplicity and non-accountability of the Federal Parole Board. It also dared to link crimes against domestic prisoners to crimes against Vietnamese prisoners, recalled the nefarious Tiger Cages on Con Son, sought to join hands with others across bars, barbed wire and free-fire zones, to assert solidarity in pain and hope of redress. There were in the leaflet no threats, no hint of violence. The 11 merely said, we have grievances, we will not take food until our grievances are taken seriously.

A month has gone by. The 11 have been taken seriously, at least by some. As they went on fasting, their friends gathered, measures were agreed on. Violence, which finds America perennially ready and able, did not occur. Non-violence, which finds America perennially unready and unable, continued. The 11 persevered in spite of a great show of force which masked a great measure of fear. Facing them was the fear of the armed bully whose knees turn to water in the presence of the unarmed man of peace. They feared not at all; they have prevailed.

As for myself, I was, as one might say, more than remotely concerned in this matter. My brothers were fasting. More than that, they were fasting for me. We had decided to use my case as an exemplary one: not because the refusal of my parole is more outrageous than that of others. In fact the faceless, unaccountable parole board had dealt inhumanly with a thousand other prisoners, and nothing was said. They had refused parole to many and granted it to few, with the mindless abandon of little men with big salaries, big power and small conscience. They had gotten away with it all; no one asked the score, no one demanded an accounting.

But my case might help, because my name and crime were known here and there. My case even stirs the public to look more closely at agents of crime and the agents of punishment.

It would seem that at least in measure, this hope has been vindicated. Eleven prisoners, bullied, segregated, harassed, transported, have stood firm. At length, their non-violent consistent purpose has moved the public, at least a little. It has moved the Congress, at least a little. One may even hope that soon the Congress may declare in effect that the human rights of prisoners do not cease to exist at the pleasure of their keepers, that 22,000 federal prisoners are no longer to be men without a country, men without a bill of rights, men without hope.

There is but one thing more to say. My brother and I did not come to prison in order to reform the prisons, or to correct the injustices of the Federal Parole Board. We came to prison as an act of resistance against the war. And the government was acute enough to take us seriously. First, it sent us to prison for a number of years. And when we continued to resist in prison, when we refused to become cheerful robots or housebroken "model inmates," the government responded in two ways. First, it named my brother in yet one more tawdry and absurd indictment. Secondly, it refused parole to both of us.

We could hardly have been paid a greater compliment. For indeed we are dangerous—dangerous to the warmaking state, dangerous in our unbroken will, dangerous in our non-violence.

We wish to link today the fast of the Danbury 11 and the continuing struggle of all who resist the war. The fate of prisoners, the fate of America, and fate of Vietnam are joined. Human rights will be denied Americans as long as the rights of man are denied the Vietnamese. The political charade in Saigon will be matched by the political charade in D.C. Thus, the ironic revenge of history; thus the war comes home.

The 11 wish to bring the peace home. To bring the peace home to men's hearts and minds, home to our churches and universities, to our economy, to the White House and the Pentagon.

Resist the war, remember the prisoners.

End the war, free the prisoners.

A Meditation from Catonsville

Every page that deals, as this one tries to, with the news about today, finds itself fairly buried before it is born. Last week's omelette. This week is still in the egg shells. I sit here, breaking eggs to make an Easter, to feed the living, as I hope, good news for bad.

Some 10 or 12 of us (the number is still uncertain) will, if all goes well (ill?), take our religious bodies during this week to a draft center in or near Baltimore. There we shall, of purpose and forethought, remove the 1-A files, sprinkle them in the public street with home-made napalm, and set them afire. For which act we shall, beyond doubt, be placed behind bars for some portion of our natural lives, in consequence of our inability to live and die content in the plagued city, to say "peace, peace" when there is no peace, to keep the poor poor, the homeless, the thirsty and hungry homeless, thirsty and hungry.

Our apologies, good friends, for the fracture of good order, the burning of paper instead of children, the angering of the orderlies in the front parlor of the charnel house. We could not, so help us God, do otherwise. For we are sick at heart; our hearts give us no rest for thinking of the Land of Burning Children. And for thinking of that other Child, of whom the poet Luke speaks. The infant was taken up in the arms of an old man, whose tongue grew resonant and vatic at the touch of that beauty. And the old man spoke: this child is set for the fall and rise of many in Israel, a sign that is spoken against.

Small consolation; a child born to make trouble, and to die for it, the First Jew (not the last) to be subject of a "definitive solution." He sets up the cross and dies on it; in the Rose Garden of the executive mansion, on the D.C. Mall, in the courtyard of the Pentagon. We see the sign, we read the direction: you must bear with us, for his sake. Or if you will not, the consequences are our own.

For it will be easy, after all, to discredit us. Our record is bad; troublemakers in church and state, a priest married despite his vows, two convicted felons. We have jail records, we have been turbulent, uncharitable, we have failed in love for the brethren, have yielded to fear and despair and pride, often in our lives. Forgive us.

We are no more, when the truth is told, than ignorant beset men, jockeying against all chance, at the hour of death, for a place at the right hand of the dying one.

We act against the law at a time of the Poor People's March, at a time moreover when the government is announcing ever more massive para-military means to confront disorder in the cities. It is announced that a computerized center is being built in the Pentagon at a cost of some seven millions of dollars, to offer instant response to outbreaks anywhere in the land; that, moreover, the government takes so serious a view of civil disorder that federal troops, with war experience in Vietnam, will have first responsibility to quell civil disorder.

The implications of all this must strike horror in the mind of any thinking man. The war in Vietnam is more and more literally brought home to us. Its inmost meaning strikes the American ghettos, in servitude to the affluent. We must resist and protest this crime.

Finally, we stretch out our hands to our brothers throughout the world. We who are priests, to our fellow priests. All of us who act against the law turn to the poor of the world, to the Vietnamese, to the victims, to the soldiers who kill and die, for the wrong reasons, for no reason at all, because they were so ordered—by the authorities of that public order which is in effect a massive institutionalized disorder.

We say: killing is disorder, life and gentleness and community and unselfishness is the only order we recognize. For the sake of that order, we risk our liberty, our good name. The time is past when good men can remain silent, when obedience can segregate men from public risk, when the poor can die without defense.

We ask our fellow Christians to consider in their hearts a question which has tortured us, night and day, since the war began. How many must die before our voices are heard, how many must be tortured, dislocated, starved, maddened? How long must the world's resources be raped in the service of legalized murder? When, at what point, will you say no to this war?

We have chosen to say, with the gift of our liberty, if necessary our lives: the violence stops here, the death stops here, the suppression of the truth stops here, this war stops here.

We wish also to place in question, by this act, all suppositions about normal times, about longings for an untroubled life in a somnolent church, about a neat timetable of ecclesiastical renewal which, in respect to the needs of men, amounts to another form of time-serving.

Redeem the times! The times are inexpressibly evil. Christians pay conscious, indeed religious tribute, to Caesar and Mars: by the approval of overkill tactics, by brinkmanship, by nuclear liturgies, by racism, by support of genocide. They embrace their society with all their heart, and abandon the cross. They pay lip service to Christ and military service to the powers of death.

And yet, and yet, the times are inexhaustibly good, solaced by the courage and hope of many. The truth rules; Christ is not forsaken. In a time of death, some men—the resisters, those who work hardily for social change, those who preach and embrace the unpalatable truth—such men overcome death, their lives are bathed in the light of the resurrection, the truth has set them free. In the jaws of death, of contumely, of good and ill report, they proclaim their love of the brethren.

We think of such men, in the world, in our nation, in the churches; and the stone in our breast is dissolved; we take heart once more.

OTHER WORKS BY DANIEL BERRIGAN, S.J.

The Dark Night of Resistance (Garden City, N.Y.: Doubleday, 1971).
No Bars to Manhood (Garden City, N.Y.: Doubleday, 1970).
The Trial of the Catonsville Nine (Boston: Beacon Press, 1970).
Crime Trial (poems) (Boston: Impressions Workshop, 1970).
They Call Us Dead Men (New York: Macmillan, 1966).

3 *Philip Berrigan, S.S.J.*

Father Philip Berrigan was the first priest in the United States to be imprisoned for his religious-political activity. Prior to his involvement with anti-war activities he spent many years working with blacks in the Baltimore ghetto. It was this experience that led him to an understanding of the repressive nature of our society's institutes and to a strong opposition to the Vietnam war. He and eight others were indicted in 1971 on conspiracy charges, the original indictment vocalized by the late F.B.I. Director, J. Edgar Hoover—in a charge which was rejected by the jury in Harrisburg, Pennsylvania.

This is an open letter to Bishop William Baum, who was recently called by the Pope to Rome to take part in the Bishops' Synod. Bishop Baum had asked for some reflections on priesthood, world justice and peace, which Father Berrigan answers in this letter.

An Open Letter to a Bishop

Here are the few ideas I promised you. They are qualified, of course, by my status and by the two years I have already served. But I possessed them before imprisonment, my books are full of them, and, it goes without saying, I believe them profoundly enough to stake my life on them. I have not found many men who can say that about their ideas.

So if you find the following negative, caustic, angry—remember that they come from one who has questioned domestic racism and modern war for ten years; who has lived in the slums and seen the

17

anguish of the poor; who has resisted militarism and war-making repeatedly; who has experienced not only prison but solitary confinement and long fasts; who has endured the charade of three political trials and who faces a fourth; and who probably will be in and out of prison for the remainder of his life. In sum, my experience has been out of the ordinary, and it comes purely from attempts to answer the question, "What does Christ ask of me?"

Despite the fact that we come from different frames of reference, and that the Berrigan view of the Gospel (Dan's and mine) is radically different from the hierarchy's, we will not admit that our own responsibilities differ from yours. In fact, we might imply that the Bishops have a deeper obligation to costly witness than we do because of the magisterium, their pastorship and charism. I tend to state the matter bluntly. On the issue of modern war, the hierarchy's default is very nearly total; it is so bad, in effect, that nuclear exchange would find Bishops unprepared to discuss anything but the morality of defending a shelter with a shotgun.

Apart from these observations, which I offer only in introduction, please convey our love and fraternity (Dan's and mine) to the Pope. It strikes me that we speak for those unable to do so, those sisters and brothers imprisoned around the world—priests, religious, laity—in Latin America, Africa, Europe, Indochina, the Marxist world. We constitute the Church in chains—advocates of resistance to naked power, disproportionate wealth, racism, warmaking. We want to express our fidelity to the Church and to the Chair of Peter, even as we sorrow over Christian myopia, hardness of heart and even cowardice.

With these preliminaries, let me offer a few general observations as well. It impresses me that thinking in the Church today, now that we are over the Vatican II euphoria, is stereotyped, cautious, quasi-despairing. Bishops, theologians, and clergy are obviously operating under the housekeeping assumption: from top to bottom, from Rome to parish, more synods, councils, democracy, and guitars will see us through present world crises. We operate as though, under a divine and magical star, we will muckle through with minimal losses while grace and providence work for us—providing, however, we pretend hard enough that nuclear overkill does not exist, that genocide in Indochina has not been carried out, that the North Atlantic community does not control

50 percent of the world's wealth, that wealth and power are not identified with the white world, and poverty and desperation are not identified with the so-called colored world.

Those Catholics—clergy and laity—who have not expressed disillusionment with such realities by leaving the Church altogether are leisurely marking time, maintaining low profile, avoiding controversy, shoring up obsolescent structures, talking a species of ecclesiastical doublespeak, and rejecting any involvement in the social horrors of the day. Apparently they take lightly the admonition of a witness like Paul: "Bear the burdens of one another, and you will have fulfilled the law (of Christ)."

Implicit in attitudes like these, shockingly pervasive as they are, is a dreadful and ill-defined fear—fear that we're not going to make it; fear that the Church will go down with the Powers of this world; fear of questioning, initiative, creativity, courage; fear of sacrifice, loneliness, criticism; fear finally of self, of neighbor, of Gospel, of Christ. (I remember President Johnson saying, with an off-the-cuff honesty quite foreign to him: "Peace is going to demand more than we counted on!") In the same manner, Catholics are discovering that Christ will demand more than we counted on. And generally, the thought fills them with dread.

The Church in America—in fact, in the West as a whole—has accepted as religion a kind of cultural syncretism, culminating in near-perfect allegiance to the State. Not a few of its more prominent Bishops have even waited upon the Presidency like court jesters. And now the culture is being violently challenged, and the State doesn't so much govern as rule by force. To whom do we turn?

A case in point is the Catholic response to the Indochinese war. It is a classic case of burning incense to Caesar. After twenty-two years' involvement in Indochina (President Truman committed American support to the French in 1949); after millions of Indochinese deaths (6 to 8 might be a conservative estimate); after as many as 100,000 American dead (Pentagon figures are probably half the total); after war expenditures of 300 billion; after documented ecocide and genocide; after all this, thirty-two American Bishops have finally condemned the immorality of the war. (This was written before the Bishops' statement of November, 1971.— Ed.) In a tragedy of this magnitude, worldwide in its ramifications, the American Church, supposedly the most vital expression of universal Catholicism, has mustered 32 tepid, episcopal voices, most of them recent. This, despite crushing evidence of the war's illegality—United Nations Charter, Geneva Accords, the SEATO agreement, the U.S. Constitution. Why so long for episcopal word, why so late and feeble? So late, in fact, that few listen and few care.

We have obviously surpassed the German Church in negligence both moral and criminal. (Resistance to Hitler, for example, meant totalitarian reprisal, which is not the case here.) Despite the clarity of Paul VI's stand, despite Constitutional protections, no Bishop has challenged the illegality of the war in serious fashion; no Bishop has broken patently immoral laws (the Apostles were martyred for refusing to obey the law); no Bishop (except Parrilla of Puerto Rico) has advocated non-violent resistance to the war (Mayor Lindsay of New York City, a nebulous liberal at best, advocated such a course two years ago). And only two or three Bishops have visited Catholic resisters in jail, at least two of them virtually apologizing for their action: "This visit is a spiritual work of mercy, which I would perform for any of my flock." More to the point would be an explanation of why they themselves were not in jail.

Furthermore, no Bishop has questioned the marriage of Big Business and Big Military in Big Government, and how the marriage results in government by and for the wealthy and powerful. No Bishop has condemned the American rape of the developing world, nor the arms race in horror weapons, nor American arms salesmanship, nor the division of the world by superpowers.

On the contrary, the American episcopacy has docilely and silently stood by while their countrymen and spiritual sons established the American empire and ruled it with ruthless might. They stood by as spectator, or advocate, while their country plunged into perpetual hot and cold warring, spent 1¼ trillion dollars on war and weapons since 1946, and filled up Arlington Cemetery with the dead of Korea, the Dominican Republic, and Indochina. And yet, the Church they lead, like the Savior, is come "to give life, and to give it more abundantly." What a gross irony!

Do I exaggerate? Perhaps. Some Catholics, who have suffered for dedication to Gospel and Church, would go much further, however. One layman I know, a superb student of Gospel politics and Gandhian non-violence, currently in jail, would say this with a snort: "Shepherds? There is not one in the American Church! They are upper-management people for the most part. And they are the State's sheep!" Of him, I must say that he is capable of transcending mediocrity. He remains loyal in a sense that most Catholics and most Bishops cannot understand.

Perhaps in the above you might perceive my difficulty in speculating about the priesthood, and how it might serve man as physician and prophet. For who will finally legislate as to training, experience, freedom? And who will provide what is most crucial of all—example? The men and women who can address the subject realistically are concerned mainly with witnessing against institutionalized terror and death—and they are in severe jeopardy or in jail.

Moreover, there is this factor to consider. If Dan and I can serve as examples of repression by the Church—for nearly ten years now we have engaged in a constant, painful, running skirmish with Church authority, encountering ridicule, outrage, exile, reassignment, mistrust—the scales have, nevertheless, slowly balanced out. Today the episcopacy tolerates us, under the jurisdiction of the State. But episcopal hypocrisy has cut very deeply. Catholics who are today developing for themselves and their brothers "the freedom with which Christ has made us free," are extremely skeptical of Papal or episcopal pronouncements. They even tend to ignore them as shallow and devious. They want the pronouncement of action, feeling that it is very late for words.

In effect, thinking Catholics make little distinction between treatment by Church and State. They know that both desire malleability and conformity, that both fear conscience, that both are self-righteous and dogmatic, that both are ruthless in handling deviants. To be fair, the Church is quicker to forgive and to forget. On the other hand, the State may be quicker to learn. But the point is that Catholics increasingly tend to ignore the official Church since it says so little real about the questions of life and death, and lives less than it says. How could it be otherwise? they ask. The official Church is not about the Gospel, or the plight of what Pope John called "the majority of men." Therefore, how can it speak to either issue?

The understanding from this quarter is simply this: both Church and State are vast, sprawling bureaucracies which share an insufferably arrogant assumption that *they* offer the fundamental answers to the human condition. The understanding, further, is that, despite claims to the contrary, Church and State have brought Western civilization to its nadir, and have destroyed other civilizations in the process.

Critics have learned, or are learning in swelling numbers from history as well as from the Gospels, that nothing much makes sense except death to self and conversion to Christ and neighbor. All the virtues exemplified by the Lord—poverty, freedom in responsibility, the politics of community, willingness to risk jail and death for the exploited person—all these attack head-on the conceptions and realities of bureaucracies whether in Church or State. The goals of bureaucracies are simply not the goals of Christ.

To apply all this seriously to contemporary problems of priesthood—especially as an American—is enormously difficult, simply because we are so cut off from the mind and life of Christ. About all one can do is fumble with a few critical questions, and then labor with the complications of response.

The Catholic priest in America—and in the West generally—is more of a cultural phenomenon than he is a Gospel man. He is a nationalistic, white supremacist, and uncritical toward affluence and its source. His training reflects nuances of these cultural fixations, but, beyond that, it schools him merely in neutrality toward life. By that I mean, he tends to take a purely institutional view of threats to life, whether they be its abuse or destruction. Indeed, if he is sensitive, he will go through immense convolutions to escape such brutalities. Or if he is hardened, he will advocate them, or remain casual in face of them.

Therefore the problem becomes—how to instill convictions strong enough to resist dehumanization in oneself, in others, in structures. How to instruct him in non-violence as a way of life, as mark of the new man, as instrument of human revolution and social regeneration? How to teach him the realities of power in all its nuances, from the will to dominate others to the will to exploit whole nations and peoples? How to toughen him so that one will understand and accept persecution, contempt, ostracism, jail, or death on account of conscience and (above all) on account of the suffering brother? How to infuse him with such sensitivity to human rights and dignity that one will confront violence in every turn of his life—in himself, in the culture, in the State? How to convince him that Christ's man must integrate word and act, in full recognition that this might lead him to death, even as it did his Lord?

I don't know, because one can neither teach the above nor administer it. But the Church can beg the grace of God, the Church can provide the setting; even though it be modern catacombs, the Church can begin, realizing that her life must always constitute beginnings, and never endings. And if such fidelity means a vocation of opposition to Powers and Principalities as they operate in government and in the circle of prestige for which the government exists, so be it. If it means the outlawry of the Church, persecution . . . the Lord spoke of that too: "The time will come when those who kill you will think they are doing a service to God." But in the process, the Church would serve humanity, would even help to give humanity a future on this planet which it could not otherwise have.

As for the impending deliberations on world justice and peace, I have anguished questions about them. Do the American Bishops accept the implications of their country's control over one-half the world's productive capacity and finance? Do they realize that, despite our affluence, we have institutionalized poverty for perhaps one-quarter of our own people, plus millions in the developing world? Will they admit that these appalling realities are not an accident, but a cold calculation, that they follow the logic of profit and policy? Can they comprehend that war, particularly modern war, decides what nation or "security bloc" will control the profits, and that on the success or failure of the Indochinese war hinges the American Open Door to the developing world? (Policy-makers fear that if the Indochinese force us out, certainty will spread among the world's poor that wars of liberation can succeed.) Do they understand that a few hundred American corporations, with hundreds of billions in assets and international holdings, are empires in their own right, exerting political and economic dominion wherever they are? To deliberate justice and peace while overlooking such realities is both ignorant and dishonest. Just as it is dishonest to deny that while most men starve, most Bishops live in comfort and affluence, welcome the dividends of offending corporations, and remain discreetly silent before the excesses of capitalism.

In closing, I hope and pray this letter is a source of help to you, and not a cause for pain and shock. You are an unusual man and Christian—intelligent, open, compassionate. Obviously you love the Church as I do. But before the tragedy and ruin of the times we must love the Church even more—enough to criticize honestly and charitably, enough to pick up heavier burdens, enough to lose everything in order that others might discover life. In essence, what would the wretched of the earth have us do to offer them hope, to lift from them the horror of war and starvation, to extend a sense of dignity and destiny in God and human community?

Our prayers go with you. And our wishes for the light, the strength, the peace of Christ.

Fraternally,
Philip Berrigan, S.S.J.

OTHER WORKS BY PHILIP BERRIGAN, S.S.J.

Prison Journals of a Priest Revolutionary (New York: Holt, Rinehart and Winston, 1971).
A Punishment for Peace (New York: Macmillan Company, 1969).
No More Strangers (New York: Macmillan Company, 1965).

4 Vinoba Bhave

Vinoba Bhave was one of Gandhi's closest and most trusted disciples. One of the most respected practitioners of non-violence in the world today, he has spent the last twenty years walking through India, begging land for the peasants of that country, and directing the land development movement. The selection here * is a translation of an article by Bhave in the journal Bhumiputra.

Christ's Teachings

Jesus Christ's teaching can be summed up in three of his sayings: 1. Love thy neighbor as thyself. 2. Love thy enemy. 3. Love one another as I have loved you.

If Jesus had merely said: "Love thy neighbor," that would have been axiomatic. If you love your neighbor, he will also love you, and if you abuse him, he too will do the same. So, to love him is in your self-interest. But Jesus added the words "as thyself." This is deep thinking, and requires great effort to practice. How much love do we lavish on ourselves, how much affection on our bodies! Lavish the same on your neighbor. So said Jesus.

This takes us to the heart of Vedanta. The same spirit that dwells within me is also in another. Therefore my love for others must equal that for myself. This I call "applied Vedanta."

The second teaching "Love thy enemy" provides a usable weapon to win the world. Mere repetition of God's name does not complete

---

* Reprinted with the permission of *Fellowship*, the magazine of the Fellowship of Reconciliation. It originally appeared in May, 1970.

25

26   PEACE AND NON-VIOLENCE

the act of devotion. One who serves God and acts according to his teaching truly worships.

Jesus therefore urged "Love thy enemy," He did not say: Love thy enemy if he loves you. That way I lose initiative to others. This limits my effectiveness. When I say I hold the initiative in the process of love, my behavior is governed by love for everyone, no matter what others do to me. Then we can conquer the world with love. Gautama Buddha said this. "Hatred is not calmed by hatred. Conquer anger with love."

Gandhi's "satyagraha" (insistence on truth) was, I believe, a practical application of this principle. He said: "We oppose evil, not the evil-doer." He left a legacy of love for the British as much as for India. There is a tremendous potential in this teaching.

Jesus gave his third teaching to his followers toward the end. There would have been nothing new if he had merely said: "Love one another." Most religious sects say this. But Jesus added "as I have loved you," meaning, "Just as I gave my all for you, you do the same for your colleagues. Dedicate yourselves to this task." This was his last message.

This is how I have understood these great teachings, and I have been trying to live by them at all times. The world urgently needs this, for if we do not work for uniting the world, we are heading toward a catastrophe. The atomic weapons have sounded a clarion call to man to unite, or they will wipe him out.

I believe in Jesus Christ, but do not believe in circumscribing him within strictly sectarian or theological walls. To me Jesus was something far beyond any individual phenomenon. He was Love and Compassion incarnate. We can carry his message to the people by serving them with love, mercy and compassion in our hearts. That message will spread despite you and me, because it is the innermost cry of the human heart. It is not necessary to make Christianity an exclusive faith by insisting that through Jesus alone humanity can realize God. Religion must be all-embracing and all-pervading. The same consolation we get from the name of Jesus should be obtainable through the names of Buddha, Mohammed or Rama.

To unite hearts is therefore the most important task before us today.

OTHER WORKS BY VINOBA BHAVE

Talks on the Gita (New York: Macmillan, 1960).
Revolutionary Sarvodaya (A Philosophy for the Remaking of Man) (Bombay: Bharatiya Vidya Bhavan Press, 1964).
Swarajyasastia (The Principles of a Nonviolent Political Order) (Bombay: Padina Publishers, 1945).
Christ: The Love Incarnate (Varanase, India: Sarva Seva Samph Prakashan, 1964).

5 Dietrich Bonhoeffer

Dietrich Bonhoeffer was the Lutheran pastor executed by Hitler for his resistance activities. A deeply religious, committed man, Bonhoeffer's writings remain a challenge and inspiration to a new generation of committed men and women. This excerpt is from Letters and Papers from Prison, *a collection of his works.**

Stations on the Road to Freedom

Discipline

If you set out to seek freedom, then learn above all things
to govern your soul and your senses, for fear that your passions
and longing may lead you away from the path you should follow.
Chaste be your mind and your body, and both in subjection,
obediently, steadfastly seeking the aim set before them;
only through discipline may a man learn to be free.

Action

Daring to do what is right, not what fancy may tell you,
valiantly grasping occasions, not cravenly doubting—
freedom comes only through deeds, not through thoughts taking
      wing.
Faint not nor fear, but go out to the storm and the action,

* Reprinted from *Letters and Papers from Prison.* Copyright The Macmillan Company, 1953, and © SCM Press Ltd., 1967.

trusting in God whose commandment you faithfully follow;
freedom, exultant, will welcome your spirit with joy.

Suffering

A change has come indeed. Your hands, so strong and active,
are bound; in helplessness now you see your action
is ended; you sigh in relief, your cause committing
to stronger hands; so now you may rest contented.
Only for one blissful moment could you draw near to touch
      freedom;
then, that it might be perfected in glory, you gave it to God.

Death

Come now, thou greatest of feasts on the journey to freedom
      eternal;
death, cast aside all the burdensome chains, and demolish
the walls of our temporal body, the walls of our souls that are
      blinded,
so that at last we may see that which here remains hidden.
Freedom, how long we have sought thee in discipline, action, and
      suffering;
dying, we now may behold thee revealed in the Lord.

OTHER WORKS BY DIETRICH BONHOEFFER

Cost of Discipleship (New York: Macmillan, 1948).
I Loved This People (Richmond, Va.: John Knox Press, 1965).
Christ the Center (New York: Harper and Row, 1966).
The Way to Freedom (New York: Harper and Row, 1966).
Ethics, Eberhard Bethge, ed. (New York: Macmillan, 1955).

6 *Dom Helder Camara*

Dom Helder Camara, the Archbishop of Recife, Brazil, is one of the most respected spokesmen for non-violent revolution in the world today. His refusal to allow violence as a means for social change is most convincing, since his experience has been with the oppressed of the Third World. The following selection * is the text of a talk delivered in Geneva in January 1970 to the World Council of Church's Consultation on Ecumenical Assistance for Development Projects.

Fetters of Injustice

You have the joy of being men of faith, Christians. It is therefore important that I tell you that this message of mine is the outcome of prayer and personal intercession. Just because it sums up a great deal of my own experience as a shepherd in the Church in the northeast of Brazil (one of the most discussed and most traumatized places in the world), I asked Christ *not* to let me transmit a view which is too impassioned and too personal.

There are far more than two or three of us gathered here in his name; the master is therefore here in our midst. In every thought and word I shall bear in mind that he is present with us, listening to us, and that he will judge the statements that we make and the proposals that we submit.

I thank our Father for this atmosphere of faith, which enables me to speak to you as if I were standing before the supreme judge and rendering account to him of my thoughts, words, actions and omissions, when speaking to you about "development projects and concern for structural changes."

* Reprinted by permission of the World Council of Churches (Geneva, 1970).

The present situation of mankind may be described briefly and objectively as follows: a sad reality, with marvelous prospects, yet the possibility (even the probability) of a tragic conclusion.

It is a sad fact that, according to the statement of the Beirut Conference (1968), 80% of the world's resources are at the disposal of 20% of the world's inhabitants: "While one segment of humanity is rich and growing richer, the rest will struggle in varying degrees of poverty and have little certainty of breaking out of their stagnation in the next decades."

The prospects are marvelous because, as we all know, for the first time in history, man is in a position to fulfill the command of the creator to dominate nature and to complete his work of creation. For the first time the technological resources available could enable us "to promote the good of every man and of the whole man."

The conclusion may be (and probably will be) tragic, owing to the blindness of the privileged 20% of mankind, who think it "normal" to spend 150 billion dollars per annum on armaments, but can hardly scrape together 10 billion for economic and social cooperation (to quote again from the Beirut Report).

Our responsibility as Christians makes us tremble. The northern hemisphere, the developed area of the world, the 20% who possess 80% of the world's resources, are of Christian origin. What impression can our African and Asian brethren and the masses in Latin America have of Christianity, if the tree is to be judged by its fruits? For we Christians are largely responsibile for the unjust world in which we live. . . .

Christianity is invoked in order to lead a sort of crusade against Communism. Christianity is invoked in order to combat the wave of hatred, deep-rooted resentment and terror which is rising everywhere. But what do the 20% who let 80% stagnate in a situation which is often sub-human—what right have they to allege that Communism crushes the human person? The 20% who are keeping 80% in a situation which is often sub-human—are they or are they not responsible for the violence and hatred which are beginning to break out all over the world?

During the course of centuries the injustices have become more and more firmly entrenched, and have perpetuated themselves to such an extent that we have come to accept them as the "social order" which should be defended and safeguarded. While all this was going on, we Christians have detached ourselves from the problems of this world to such an extent that we have made it easier for injustice to take root.

Even sadder than this is the spectacle presented by us, Christians, torn by our struggles and dissensions which destroy the seamless robe of Christ.

Nevertheless, it is easier for Christians of different denominations to cooperate in an effort to assist man (which is one of the commandments laid upon us by the Gospel) than it is to unite around the eucharistic table, or even to unite in hearing the Word of God.

What a splendid testimony we could give if we were to unite with our Christian brethren in the developed countries to do everything in our power to overcome the egoism of the northern hemisphere—which is the Christian hemisphere, or at any rate Christian in origin! We should do our utmost to influence the northern hemisphere to re-examine the implications of justice in its relations with the underdeveloped countries.

What splendid testimony we could give to our non-Christian brethren in Africa and Asia, and to the masses in Latin America (who are more easily moved by feeling than by personal conviction) if we were to unite, so as to try to carry out the fine convictions expressed in the reports from Medellin (meeting of the Catholic hierarchy of Latin America), Uppsala (Fourth Assembly of the World Council of Churches) and Beirut (Conference on World Cooperation for Development organized by the World Council of Churches and the Pontifical Commission "Justice and Peace"). If we add the encyclical *Populorum Progressio* of Pope Paul VI, we can say that for the next few years we Christians do not require any more documents concerning the social sphere. The problem that we now have to tackle is that of putting our fine theories into practice.

This is where the difficulties arise, both externally and internally. Usually the privileged 20%, and their governments, welcome effusively documents like those mentioned above, and say that they are in complete agreement with them. But as soon as someone decides to apply these documents (to which so much tribute is paid), he is immediately accused of being subversive and of being a Communist.

Everyone agrees that abuses and wrongs exist in the socio-economic and politico-cultural structures. But (say the governments and the privileged section of the population), it is impossible in a few days, a few months, or even a few years to change things which have taken centuries to build up. Many Christian leaders are deterred by the fear that if changes are too rapid they may upset the "social order," undermine the principle of authority and destroy private ownership.

Division starts within the Church itself, then: disagreement between the cautious, moderate people who want quiet, unhurried change, and those who feel that there is no time to be lost because we must catch up on centuries of stagnation, and should confess serious sins of omission. The *social order?* What social order are people talking about? The one that we see today, that consists in leaving millions of God's children in miserable poverty, should rather be called *social disorder,* systematized injustice. *Private ownership?* Is it not evident to everyone that on this point we Christians have abandoned the Fathers of the Church, and that we have ended by attributing divine right to private ownership, whereas God's law says that the wealth of the world should be shared by all, and should never form odious, oppressive monopolies?

One allegation also made by the privileged section and by governments is that the documents issued by the Church demanding structural changes are extremely vague; they lose themselves in generalizations instead of indicating concrete solutions. This objection alarms some Christians, because they fear that denouncing what is wrong and urging structural changes without giving concrete indications for action is preparing the way for agitators and Communists.

You have certainly observed what follies and cruelties are committed on the pretext of preventing subversion and combatting Communism.

The first consequence is that existing structures are maintained— structures in which centuries of violence are entrenched, for they protect the privileges of a minority at the expense of the poverty of millions. Totalitarian methods are adopted; informers are encouraged; everyone suspects everyone else; liberty is completely suspended, including freedom of speech. The atmosphere is one of complete insecurity, arbitrary imprisonment; moral and physical torture are employed in order to extort confessions. Do not think that I am alluding simply to one country; the serious fact is that the anti-Communist obsession everywhere leads logically to these methods which, in turn, lead to ever-increasing antagonism and violence.

Anyone who is sincerely democratic, who believes in the power of truth and love and wants to speak, is unable to do so, for he is unable to write or to hold meetings. His intentions are misinterpreted and he has no opportunity to state the truth. It is impossible to get a hearing for what political prisoners say or what they have said. Surely it is easy to understand why young people especially resort to clandestine action and try to combat violence with violence.

At this point perhaps it is possible to envisage the role (possibly a decisive one) which the World Council of Churches and the Papal Commission "Justice and Peace" may be called to play in God's plans, as the conscience of the really free world, and as the mouthpiece of those who cannot speak for themselves.

It is not by chance that we, as Christians, are so closely concerned with the problem of the distance, daily more striking, between the developed and the underdeveloped world. Let us have the humility and the courage to acknowledge that we are, to a large extent, responsible for allowing injustice between men to have reached such a point, since this injustice stems from the hemisphere which, at least in origin, is Christian. The simple fact is that we should atone for our sins of omission.

Injustice is the right word to use. In the developed countries, when one is thinking about the poorer countries, the temptation is to imagine that basically the problem is a racial one (there are whites and then . . . the others—black, yellow and mulatto—in the rest of the world), a racial problem aggravated by a certain unwillingness to come to terms with it, by dishonesty, and above all, recently, by the demographic explosion. We could debate these views and prejudices one by one. However, even if some of the questions raised were valid, this should not be a pretext for forgetting that there exist places in the world where key decisions are made, imperial capitals where international economic policies are drawn up, where prices are fixed, where measures are taken whereby the rich countries always become richer and the poor countries always poorer.

It is easy and convenient for the rich countries, when face to face with the poorer countries, to think in terms of financial and technical aid, programs whose result, nearly always, is that the aid is merely apparent and leads to the actual despoiling of the poorer countries. It is inconvenient for the rich countries to work out effective changes in the socio-economic, political or cultural structures of the poor countries, for the very simple reason that the latter would then no longer need to provide the raw materials essential for the administration and expansion of the developing economies.

We should not delude ourselves: a change in structure in the underdeveloped countries is not possible without a change in structure in the developed countries. The expression must be taken literally. I do not mean merely a change in mentality with regard to the poor countries. I mean a profound change in international commercial policy. How much longer are we going to permit international trusts to make small groups of men fabulously wealthy, while they keep millions of others in slavery? I do not want to be told that modern corporations are becoming democratic because millions and millions of ordinary people are becoming shareholders and thus have control over the concern. Shareholders, yes, in the sense that they hold a few meager shares, but without any say in the management of the corporation, which is carried out anonymously, impassively and coldly by a group of people who do not mind coming face to face with those they have crushed.

It is no use asserting that there are laws which control the investment of profits abroad. Who does not know that there are numerous ways of evading these laws?

It is not honest to say that the rich countries invest in the poor countries purely out of generosity and the desire to help, assuming that they have sufficient internal markets and no longer need raw materials now that there are so many substitutes.

The World Council of Churches and the Papal Commission "Justice and Peace" could set the example, during the present period of violence and deeply polarized attitudes, of using the non-violent action of the peacemakers to good effect by creating a movement of public opinion, on the European scale, which would perhaps bring moral pressure to bear, leading to a change in structure here as a prior condition to bringing about a change in structure of the underdeveloped countries.

Just imagine that the World Council and the Papal Commission were to arrange for a basic document to be drawn up by experts, summarizing the principal points of the reports of the first three conferences of the United Nations Conference on Trade and Development.

We all know that the three conferences of UNCTAD—two of which took place here in Geneva—constitute the most important steps taken by the underdeveloped world to bring about a recognition of its rights with regard to the developed world. And we also all know how the USA and the USSR, typical representatives of capitalist and socialist countries, both showed an equal lack of sensibility and comprehension when confronted by countries concerned with rising out of their misery.

This basic document summarizing the UNCTAD reports should be sent by the World Council and the Papal Commission to the principal European universities on both sides of the Iron Curtain, inviting them to a seminar, at which would be decided once and for all whether, on the world scale, relations between countries of plenty and countries of poverty are just or unjust.

A meeting of experts from the principal European universities would cause a stir and attract representatives of the media, both written and spoken, of the whole continent. The World Council and the Papal Commission could be prepared to:

—point out that the press in the developed countries has already gone beyond the stage at which, on the whole, it only described the folklore of the countries of the Third World; today it has made the entire world realize that famine, poverty and underdevelopment do in fact exist;

—supply details enabling one to follow more closely the university debate on the essential relationships between developed and underdeveloped countries.

The World Council and the Papal Commission would profit by inviting key persons of the main world religions. As all religions have a direct and vital interest in world peace, they should be shown to what extent peace is compromised by injustices on a world-wide scale. The religions would be asked to unite and to bring all the moral force they possess to work toward an achievement of justice, the prime condition for peace.

Here are a few other possibilities:

—a meeting of the leaders of all the main political parties in Europe;

—a meeting of the heads of business concerns and leaders of trade unions, with effective repercussions in their respective classes;
—a meeting of experts in techniques and structures, the probable technocrats of tomorrow.

Far be it for us to forget that God exists and that he has and always will have the right of interfering in the natural order.

We bear witness to the fact that our creator and Father wished us to be formed in his image and likeness and charged us to hold sway over nature and complete the creation.

When you ask if it is possible to quote the example of a country which, without armed violence, has been able to change its structures, it is possible to reply that up until very recently, humanity did not possess the powerful means of social communication which we have today.

However, it so happens that in underdeveloped countries, those who wish to upset the existing structures, even if they use democratic methods, lose access to these powerful means of social communication, even if, at the same time, they do not lose their civil rights.

Therefore, let us render this service in the cause of peace: without measuring the sacrifices, try to prove that truth, love and faith, with the divine blessing, are capable of moving and breaking down the walls of Jericho.

OTHER WORKS BY DOM HELDER CAMARA

Revolution Through Peace (New York: Harper and Row, 1971).
Spiral of Violence (London: Sheed and Ward, 1969).
Church and Colonialism (London: Sheed and Ward, 1969).

7 Cesar Chavez

Dynamic, charismatic, deeply committed and deeply religious, Cesar Chavez is the leader of an unprecedented strike among migrant workers in California. Chavez is not a philosopher; he is an activist. It is through these actions that one can see a non-violence that is deeply rooted in his faith.

The first selection * discusses the need for creativity in using non-violence as a method for social change. The second selection * is the text of a statement that was made by Chavez at the completion of his twenty-five-day penitential fast in Delano, California, March 10, 1968.

Creative Non-Violence

Many people feel that an organization that uses non-violent methods to reach its objectives must continue winning victories one after another in order to remain non-violent. If that be the case, then a lot of efforts have been miserable failures. There is a great deal more involved than victories. My experience has been that the poor know violence more intimately than most people because it has been a part of their lives, whether the violence of the gun or the violence of want and need.

I don't subscribe to the belief that non-violence is cowardice, as some militant groups are saying. In some instances non-violence requires more militancy than violence. Non-violence forces you to

* Reprinted with the permission of the United Farmworkers Organizing Committee.

38

abandon the short-cut in trying to make a change in the social order. Violence, the short-cut, is the trap people fall into when they begin to feel that it is the only way to attain their goal. When these people turn to violence, it is a very savage kind.

When people are involved in something constructive, trying to bring about change, they tend to be less violent than those who are not engaged in rebuilding or in anything creative. Non-violence forces one to be creative; it forces any leader to go to the people and get them involved so that they can come forth with new ideas. I think that once people understand the strength of non-violence—the force it generates, the love it creates, the response that it brings from the total community—they will not be willing to abandon it easily.

Statement at Completion of Fast

I undertook this fast because my heart filled with grief and pain for the suffering of farm workers. The fast was first of all for me, and then for all of us in the union. It was a fast for non-violence and a call to sacrifice.

Our struggle is not easy. Those who oppose our cause are high and powerful and they have many allies in high places. We are poor, and our allies are few—but we have something the rich do not own. We have our own bodies and spirits and the justice of our cause as our weapon.

When we are really honest with ourselves we must admit that our lives are all that really belong to us. So it is how we use our lives that determines what kind of men we are. It is my deepest belief that only by giving our lives do we find life.

I am convinced that the truest act of courage, the strongest act of manliness, is to sacrifice ourselves for others in a totally non-violent struggle for justice. To be a man is to suffer for others.

God help us to be men.

BOOKS ABOUT CESAR CHAVEZ

Mark Day, *Forty Acres: Cesar Chavez and the Farmworkers* (New York: Praeger, 1971).

Peter Matthiessen, *Sal Si Puedes: Cesar Chavez and the New American Revolution* (New York: Random House, 1969).

8 William Sloane Coffin

Rev. William Sloane Coffin is a chaplain at Yale University, and one of the first men in the nation to challenge this country's policy in Vietnam from a moral perspective. The following selection * well illustrates this view.

Militant Non-Violence

Non-violence badly needs redefinition. Non-violence should mean not only a refusal to do another physical harm, but also a determination not to violate the integrity of any human being, our own integrity included.

According to this definition we all come out pretty violent, and first of all toward ourselves. For we love policies of repression: self-denial in place of self-discovery and self-fulfillment, moralistic terrorism in place of ethical persuasion. Instead of bringing into the full light of day the ambivalences that are part of the human equipment, we hide them. In every relationship of love there is hate, in every expression of altruism some self-advantage is being sought —but instead of examining, we repress. But these policies of repression are wrong if only because the subconscious has no digestive tract. What goes down must come up, and it usually does so in the form of displaced violence. Thus older folk who violently repress their sexuality become violent when they see the present permissiveness of the young. People who repress their ethical natures become violent when others make claims on their consciences. Middle class youth becomes violent toward middle class values because it cannot quite take leave of the class it forswears.

The result is disaster. As Freud once observed acidly, "It is a good thing men do not love their neighbors as themselves; if they

* Reprinted with the permission of *Motive Magazine*, where the article first appeared in the January 1970 issue.

41

did they would kill them." And that seems to be what we're up to a good deal of the time.

The point is that it is all right to have ambivalent feelings. It is wrong to pretend not to have them. It is wrong to have pretensions of innocence when in the sullied stream of human life holiness is man's only option. As "whole" and "holy" have the same root, holiness can be defined as the effort to bring into one integrated and dedicated whole the sensual, logical and ethical aspects of our nature, our past, present and future, our race, nationality and class. And holiness is possible, given the certainty of God's love.

But let us go on with this theme of non-violence and recognize that as with individuals, so with social structures: they can be outwardly orderly yet inwardly violent. And if violence means violating human integrity, then without hesitation we must call violent any university, business, government or social structure that condemns human beings to hopelessness and helplessness, to less than human existence. Further it is clear that people concerned with non-violence must show not only compassion for the victims of violence but also a determination to change the structures of society that make them objects of compassion. Let religious folk note well Colin Williams' splendid statement that it is no longer possible to distinguish between a personal conversion experience and a change in social attitudes.

That is why Elijah was so determined, despite the personal risk, to confront Ahab. And when Ahab called him the disturber of Israel, Elijah properly retorted that it was Ahab who was the disturber of Israel's peace, for his rule rejected more than it reflected the commandments of God. In other words Ahab's kingdom was an established disorder, and as Augustine later wrote, "What are . . . kingdoms without justice but large bands of robbers?"

What we need to recognize is Gandhi's truth that exploitation is the essence of violence, that violence in its cruelest form is not blue collar or no collar, but white collar; not individual and messy, but organized and efficient, antiseptic and profitable. The violent ones are less the mugging drug addicts that inhabit slum tenements than the modern-day Ahabs who occupy pentagonal palaces, skyscrapers like the Ling Tower, the house that weapons built, and who never see blood unless their secretaries have a nosebleed.

To see how violent a world we live in, we have only to engage in an exercise of imagination: There are now three billion people on this planet. Reduce these peoples proportionately to a town of 1,000 and 60 will be Americans, 940 the rest of the world's population. The 60 Americans will control half the total income of the town. The 60 Americans will enjoy on an average fifteen times as much of all material goods as the rest of the citizens. The 60 Americans will enjoy a life expectancy of 71 years while the 940 on an average will die before they are 40.

Now we can see how ridiculous it is to define violence in physical terms alone. For a man killed by a bullet is no less dead than a man who has died from a disease resulting from eradicable poverty. When you stop to think of it, poverty is no longer inevitable; therefore it is intolerable. It is no more a private tragedy; it is now a public crime.

But there are other forms of violence and death, the kinds suffered by the 60 Americans. American production is now powerfully oriented toward consumption. And as consumption seems almost limitless, so too appears production. But to produce something, something else has to be destroyed, and the evidence of destruction is all about us. "Modern production," write two commentators, "has obscured the sun and the stars, and it has made the cities unlivable. It chews up great forests and drinks whole lakes and rivers, and it consumes men's religions and traditions and makes nonsense of their notions of the aims of education. It periodically slays heaps of men in war, and it daily mangles the spirits of millions of others in meaningless labor."

Oh for a President who could repeat, in place of clichés whose application has long since ceased, these words of the poet-king so eerie in their timeliness:

The bay trees in our country are all wither'd
And meteors fright the fixed stars of heaven;
The pale-fac'd moon looks bloody on the earth
And lean-look'd prophets whisper fearful change.

But what is to be done—non-violently? One obvious thing is to speak Elijah's truth that we dwell in a land of idol worshipers. Like Willy Loman we have the wrong dreams. The wrongness comes through most poignantly when talking with blue-collar workers who, unlike blacks today and unlike whites during the Depression, are not excluded from the American pie; they are part of the American dream. Only what kind of a dream is it to return from spirit-mangling work to payments on the car, a mortgage on the house, stultifying TV programs, an over-heated teen-age daughter and a D-in-English car-smashing son? But who, particularly in the Church, has had the candor and courage to tell them of their wrong dreams, to tell them that the wonders of man do not consist in consumer goods, to tell them that their wretchedness is interior and therefore that it is wrong to seek to scapegoat long-haired students, liberal professors, the Vietcong, the UN?

In its most dangerous form, idol worshiping is reflected in the government, and we need not bother with the obvious examples today. Like many of you I read Robert Kennedy's account of the Cuban missle crisis and was greatly impressed by the President's restraint. But the true hero of the story—if hero there be—is Nikita Khrushchev, for President Kennedy himself privately admitted (and unfortunately the admission is not in the book) that had he as an American President withdrawn missles as did Khrushchev, he would have been impeached.

Secretary Rusk succinctly summed up the story: we were eyeball to eyeball, and the other fellow blinked. Most Americans thought this kind of manliness impressive. But what impresses me is that if High Noon encounters with nuclear weapons represent manliness, then we simply have to reinvent manhood.

And this, I think, is what non-violence is really all about: a new kind, or perhaps a New Testament kind, of manhood, patterned after the person of Jesus.

I have only begun to think about this new kind of manhood, but this much at least seems clear. If the aim of non-violence is reconciliation and healing, both for the individual and society, then the emphasis must be not on being right but on being loyal to a truth that is good for all. It is not we who must prevail but a truth that is as true for our adversaries as it is for us. Clearly this demands an openness to, a willingness to learn from, our adversaries. (Actually a refusal to learn from another always reflects doubts about one's own position.) In short, the fight is for everyone. Every confrontation should offer opportunities, as Gandhi would say, "for all to rise above their present conditions." And this means we should avoid words or acts which inhibit the awakening of a decent response and only confirm us in our self-righteousness and self-pity.

It is at this point that words such as "pig," "nigger" and "honky" are not helpful. And it is at this point that physical violence is unhelpful. I can consider myself the equal of a man threatening me with violence, but I have trouble considering myself his equal if I am threatening him. (This, of course, is not to ignore the distinction between the violence of the oppressor and the violence of the oppressed.)

But openness to an adversary does not mean acquiescence in any evil in which he may be involved. Non-violence has nothing to do with passivity; it has everything to do with resistance. So if a man is opposed to the war in Vietnam, he should naturally refuse to have anything to do with it and go to jail rather than enter the Army. If he opposes the draft he should not register for it provided he has thought through all the consequences of his action for himself and others. For until the adversary in power knows that non-violent men are willing to suffer for their beliefs, he will not be truly willing to listen to them, knowing he can count on their ultimate acquiescence to his power if not to his opinion. Of this we have had endless examples in recent years.

Somehow we have to combine a quality of openness with a quality of determination. We have to fight racial and class enemies, yet never as personal enemies. We have to become twice as militant and twice as non-violent, twice as tough and twice as tender, as only the truly strong can be tender.

That is why a Communion service is so meaningful to me. "After the same manner he took the cup, after he had supped, saying, 'This cup is the new covenant in my blood.' " That's what we need—a new covenant with God and with Christ for a new kind of manhood. To this new covenant we must devote a great deal of thought. Perhaps we should inscribe on the exit doors of the church these words of Daedalus: "I go forth . . . to forge in the smith of my soul the uncreated conscience of my race."

9 *Tom Cornell*

Tom Cornell, head of the Catholic Peace Fellowship, and an associate editor of The Catholic Worker, *has been active in all forms of peace education and activism. This selection * is a statement made before sentencing at his trial in November, 1966 for destruction of his draft card. On May 27, 1968, the Supreme Court ruled 7-1 to uphold the 1965 law which makes it a crime to burn or otherwise destroy a draft card; Tom Cornell began to serve his sentence in June 1968.*

Not the Smallest Grain of Incense

The Justice Department took it all with unaccustomed gravity. The gods had been mocked, and that could not be ignored.

It is characteristic of states to gather power unto themselves. With the accumulation of power they quickly forget the source and the purpose of that power. They tend to take on divine prerogatives. God alone has dominion over human life. Yet the state usurps that dominion by exacting capital punishment and by prosecuting war, always, mind you, in self-defense.

Throughout the Old Testament there is the recurring theme of idolatry. The early Christians were well aware of it too. Less so today. I submit, Your Honor, that the state today, the Government of the United States of America, is just as much a pagan god as Caesar was in imperial Rome, and that our society is just as guilty of idolatry as the worshipers at Caesar's pagan altars. This new Moloch demands the bodies of our young men in its service, the

* Reprinted from *The Catholic Worker*, where it originally appeared.

service of death rather than the service of life, and little by little it
exacts the souls of all of us as well, so that in the name of anti-
communism and anti-totalitarianism, we are moving toward universal conscription. As part of this process, the Congress took a
small piece of paper, of no significant value to anyone but a bar-
tender, and said over it, "Hoc est enim Corpus Meum." The sacra-
ment of the state then had to be honored. So the act of burning the
draft cards was for me an act of purposeful desecration and an act
of purification. Let not any state have such trappings, or arrogate
to itself such prerogatives. It is blasphemy! I suspect that the great
public interest that was generated by this symbolic act came from
a dim awareness in the public mind that a blasphemous profana-
tion had been made of the state religion. How else explain it, that
burning an insignificant piece of paper is a crime, but that burning children in napalm is sacred duty? . . .

   Dave (Miller) went to jail yesterday. It was the most tortur-
ous and cruel court hearing I have ever witnessed. The judge
simply never got the idea. He seemed detached but anxious to make
it appear that he was willing to go as far out of his way as con-
ceivable to make an accommodation with Dave. He offered deal
after deal, offered time for Dave to talk it over with his family. Dave
very calmly and simply told him, at each point, that he had exam-
ined the alternatives and that he was not going to procure a new
card, or seek I-O status. . . .

   Marvin Karpatkin, our lawyer, pointed out the similarity of
Dave's situation with that of the Jehovah's Witnesses who were
convicted on the flag-salute thing. A term of probation for the
parents of the children was that they instruct their children to
salute the flag. Obviously they could not, and so were again subject
to punishment. Dave didn't burn the card to burn a card, but to get
rid of it and to disassociate himself from the Selective Service System. To procure a new card would be to deny his whole basis. They
make you sentence yourself! "Render unto Caesar," the judge
said. I thought of Maximilian: "You must render unto Caesar what
Caesar needs." "I will never!" said Dave, not with defiance, but
simply as a statement of fact.

   Not the smallest grain of incense on the altar. That's what that
card means to me. The smallest grain of incense. Fortunately I
didn't get any probation, just a six-month sentence. I'm really grate-

ful for such a light sentence, and feel all the worse, on the other hand, for Jim (Wilson) and Dave. You don't really know what a sentence like that is until you think of your kids. I had no idea having a little boy would mean so much to me. And we'll be having another in August. Dave's girl and Jim's boy won't know them till they're three years old! For me it will be over by next spring, probably. I don't think the government is fool enough to prosecute me for non-possession of a card after that. At least I hope not. It seems too absurd.

10 *Dorothy Day*

A Communist in her 20's and a convert to Catholicism during the Depression years, Dorothy Day is the founder and major directive force of the Catholic Worker Movement, known for its hospitality houses and rural communities. She is a humble, deeply spiritual woman who has fed the hungry, clothed the naked, and sheltered the homeless. She has nourished many of the radical Catholic figures of the day, and is known for her long-time peace witness.

The first selection * is from the Fall Appeal (there is also a Spring Appeal) that she writes for The Catholic Worker *to raise funds for her work at St. Joseph's House, 36 East First Street, New York, 10003, and was dated October 1971. The second selection * enunciates principles of the Catholic Worker Movement that have been influenced by the thought and experiences of Dorothy Day.*

Fall Appeal

Dear fellow workers whom we love: Last night three people came in a half-hour after dinner was over, and we were cleaned out. The cupboard was bare. We had meatloaf and spinach and by the time I got in from 5:30 Mass the potatoes and gravy were gone and only a cup of spinach water remained. A most healthy meal. But there were apples from the farm. God be thanked. Which meant enough apple sauce for everyone that evening and for the soup "lions," as Marge's little children used to call our guests years ago, this

* Reprinted with the permission of *The Catholic Worker*.

49

morning. As for the late late guests, we had a sack of oatmeal, quick cooking, and with margarine and sugar and coffee and apple sauce, they too were served. Another old man came in later and just wanted two slices of bread. "I have an onion," he said. Even as I was writing this a student came in and asked if he could have breakfast and supper with us. "I'm working part-time and trying to go to school; it would ease the strain if I didn't have to buy meals," he said.

Knowing the cost of one sandwich when I am traveling, I can see how much of our money goes for food for maybe sixty or seventy three-meals-a-day in town, and the soup line which goes up to 200 according to the time of month. At the farm they have grown a great amount of vegetables and there are fruit and grapes, so a hundred pound sack of brown rice or whole wheat flour makes everything go far. All this means that I am writing another appeal for help from you, our readers and co-workers. Have you ever read Knut Hamsun's *Hunger?* There is so much hunger in the world even in these times when we can grow so much food.

Hunger makes for bitterness and anger. We are living in a time of violence what with the war extended to Laos and Cambodia. There is also a reflected violence at home, which shows in our thoughts and words often.

St. Augustine has some good advice about voluntary poverty which enables us all to do the works of mercy: "Find out how much God has given you, and from it take what you need; the remainder which you do not require is needed by others. The superfluities of the rich are the necessities of the poor. Those who retain what is superfluous possess the goods of others."

To serve others, to give what we have is not enough unless we always show the utmost respect for each other and all we meet. One of the most moving things in the Attica tragedy was the insistence of the blacks that their religion be respected, the garb of the Moslem, the rejection of pork. When one thinks of the pomp of the Church in its worship—"Worship the Lord in holy attire," the Psalmist said; when one remembers that Brother Charles of Jesus was converted by seeing the faithfulness of the Moslem to prayer; when one remembers the integrity and dedication of Malcolm X after his conversion to the Moslem faith, one can only cringe at the lack of respect shown these men of Attica in their demands for religious freedom. Certainly it was one of the demands which could have been negotiated, yet their insistence in that respect for themselves and their fellows only ended in their death.

And I think too that that is what our soup line means. All the young students who live with us show their respect by doing the menial jobs, cleaning toilets, scrubbing floors, washing dishes. Men from this Bowery area also help with the mailing of the 80,000 copies of *The Catholic Worker* each month. It is a community activity, a little "industry" in which all share in the profits, those profits meaning a place to live, food, clothing, companionship, etc. Of course it is work which men need most. We are ever conscious of that. But we all have that; we are self-employed, with no bosses! And no wages! "From each according to his ability and to each according to his need." Or, as St. Paul puts it, "Let your abundance supply their want." So God bless us all, and you too, who have helped us over the years, and will again, we know.

> Love and gratitude,
> Dorothy Day

Catholic Worker Positions

The general aim of the Catholic Worker Movement is to realize in the individual and in society the expressed and implied teachings of Christ. It must, therefore, begin with an analysis of our present society to determine whether we already have an order that meets with the requirements of justice and charity of Christ.

The society in which we live and which is generally called capitalist (because of its method of producing wealth) and bourgeois (because of the prevalent mentality) is not in accord with justice and charity—

IN ECONOMICS—because the guiding principle is production for profit and because production determines needs. A just order would provide the necessities of life for all, and needs would determine what would be produced. From each according to his ability, to each according to his needs. Today we have a non-producing class which is maintained by the labor of others with the consequence that the laborer is systematically robbed of that wealth which he produces over and above what is needed for his bare maintenance.

IN PSYCHOLOGY—because capitalist society fails to take in the whole nature of man but rather regards him as an economic factor in production. He is an item in the expense sheet of the employer. Profit determines what type of work he shall do. Hence, the deadly routine of assembly lines and the whole mode of factory production. In a just order the question will be whether a certain type of work is in accord with human values, not whether it will bring a profit to the exploiters of labor.

IN MORALS—because capitalism is maintained by class war. Since the aim of the capitalist employer is to obtain labor as cheaply as possible and the aim of labor is to sell itself as dearly as possible and buy the products produced as cheaply as possible, there is an inevitable and persistent conflict which can only be overcome when the capitalist ceases to exist as a class. When there is but one class the members perform different functions but there is no longer an employer/wage-earner relationship.

TO ACHIEVE THIS SOCIETY WE ADVOCATE:

A complete rejection of the present social order and a non-violent revolution to establish an order more in accord with Christian values. This can only be done by direct action since political means have failed as a method for bringing about this society. Therefore we advocate a personalism which takes on ourselves responsibility for changing conditions to the extent that we are able to do so. By establishing Houses of Hospitality we can take care of as many of those in need as we can rather than turn them over to the impersonal "charity" of the State. We do not do this in order to patch up the wrecks of the capitalist system but rather because there is always a shared responsibility in these things and the call to minister to our brother transcends any consideration of economics. We feel that what anyone possesses beyond basic needs does not belong to him but rather to the poor who are without it.

We believe in a withdrawal from the capitalist system so far as each one is able to do so. Toward this end we favor the establishment of a *distributist economy* wherein those who have a vocation to the land will work on the farms surrounding the village itself. In this way we will have a decentralized economy which will dispense with the State as we know it and will be federationist in character as was society during certain periods that preceded the rise of national states.

We believe in worker-ownership of the means of production and distribution, as distinguished from nationalization. This is to be accomplished by decentralized co-operatives and the elimination of a distinct employer class. It is revolution from below and not (as political revolutions are) from above. It calls for widespread and universal ownership by all men of property as a stepping stone to a communism that will be in accord with the Christian teaching of detachment from material goods and which, when realized, will express itself in common ownership. "Property, the more common it is, the more holy it is," St. Gertrude writes.

We believe in the complete equality of all men as brothers under the Fatherhood of God. Racism in any form is blasphemy against God who created all mankind in his image and who offers redemption to all. Man comes to God freely or not at all and it is not the function of any man or institution to force the Faith on anyone. Persecution of any people is therefore a serious sin and denial of free will.

We believe further that the revolution that is to be pursued in ourselves and in society must be pacifist. Otherwise it will proceed by force and use means that are evil and which will never be outgrown, so that they will determine the END of the revolution and that end will again be tyranny. We believe that Christ went beyond natural ethics and the Old Dispensation in this matter of force and war and taught non-violence as a way of life. So that when we fight tyranny and injustice and the class war we must do so by spiritual weapons and by non-cooperation. Refusal to pay taxes, refusal to register for conscription, refusal to take part in civil-defense drills, non-violent strikes, withdrawal from the system are all methods that can be employed in this fight for justice.

We believe that success, as the world determines it, is not the criterion by which a movement should be judged. We must be prepared and ready to face seeming failure. The most important thing is that we adhere to these values which transcend time and for which we will be asked a personal accounting, not as to whether they succeeded (though we should hope that they do) but as to whether we remained true to them even though the whole world go otherwise.

OTHER WORKS BY DOROTHY DAY

Meditations (New York: Newman Press, 1970).
Loaves and Fishes (New York: Harper and Row, 1963).
The Long Loneliness (New York: Harper and Row, 1952).
The Catholic Worker (Westport, Conn.: Greenwood Reprint Corp., 1970).

11 *Danilo Dolci*

*Danilo Dolci went to northwestern Sicily in 1952
to work with the people there, people caught in
desperate poverty. He has sought to educate the
people to their own worth and to the effectiveness
of concerted, non-violent action (including work
strikes, public fasts and marches). Dolci and the
people themselves have begun to erode the power
of the Mafia.*

*The first selection * was submitted by Dolci to the
War Resisters' International Triennial Conference.
The second selection deals with the work of various
study centers in Sicily.*

Non-Violence
vs. the Mafia

The problem of our new revolution is to find
how best to eliminate exploitation, murder,
the investment of energy in weapons of destruction—how to pro-
voke chain reactions not of hate and death but of new constructive-
ness, of new quality of life.

It is easy to doubt the efficacy of non-violent revolution while it
has yet to be proved, historically and systematically, that it can
change *structures*. But in a world tired of murder, betrayal, pointless death, there can be a more direct appeal to people's consciences when a movement for change is both robust *and* non-
violent.

In Partinico in the winter of '55, there was really desperate

* Reprinted with the permission of *WIN* Magazine, where it originally
appeared.

hunger among most of the population, outlawed in every sense from the life of the nation. When we held the first peasant meetings, quite a few proposed flinging stones through the carabinieri's windows or setting fire to the Town Hall. But the majority objected that this way would be less effective, since people would be unwilling to participate if it meant putting themselves in the wrong. After fuller discussion, we decided on a day's fast by 1,000 people, to be followed by a "strike in reverse"—working on a dilapidated country road. The people joined in with scarcely any fear at all, despite massive intervention by the police—because they knew they weren't doing anybody any harm: and within a few days they had succeeded as never before in penetrating the public conscience with their protest and their own positive proposals.

With this profound capacity for awakening consciences, nonviolent action is also revolutionary in that it activates other forces that are revolutionary in different ways. And everyone who wants change makes the sort of revolution he can.

Often the situation in Partinico was so grave, the terror of the Mafia so widespread, that it was like working on the edge of a landslide. When some of us felt the situation demanded action, we decided to fast (as one has to in prison when it is the only action possible), in order to try to bring the peasants out of their isolation by joining with them in exposing the intolerable reality and making specific suggestions. At first many people disagreed with this method, but gradually as the days passed almost everyone's conscience was galvanized; discussions became animated; enterprises proliferated—among the embryonic trade unions, the local councils, parties, individuals and groups, often even in rivalry with one another. And many people now, as they look at the new lake with its ducks, inevitably reflect on the method which, from the first few stones to the final great mass, brought about the construction of this magnificent dam.

Sometimes we may admire violent revolutionary forces not because they are the only possible ones, or the most suitable to the circumstances, but because where they are active they are often the only ones brave enough to exist at all. But anyone who thinks war the *highest form* of struggle, or the *means* of resolving conflicts, still has a very limited vision of man. Anyone with effective revolutionary experience knows—and has to admit—that to succeed in changing a situation he must have not only a material appeal but a higher *moral* appeal; he knows that the appeal to truer principles, to a superior ethic, itself becomes an element of strength: and thus his action is revolutionary also insofar as it helps create new feelings, new abilities, new culture, new instincts—a new human nature.

Personally, I am absolutely convinced that peace means action —when necessary revolutionary, but *non-violent*. I recognize that a diseased situation can be brought nearer to health, and therefore nearer to peace, by other means too: but I know that violence, even when directed to good ends, still contains the seed of death.

Which are more numerous—those who would gain by changes, or those who think they benefit from maintaining the status quo?

There are thousands of millions of people in the world at present excluded from progress. By interpreting and expressing the profound needs of *these* people, by helping them to take stock of their problems, by helping them to initiate enterprises of every kind, at every level, and to press effectively for changes, we can activate a positively revolutionary force.

Though planning from a position of power is more likely to be effective, we musn't underestimate the possibilities of opposition planning.

Many revolutionary movements, though good at arousing consciences and effective in protest and pressure, suffer from weakness on their *constructive* front. But the demolition of old systems and the building of new organic groups should be simultaneous, co-ordinated activities which potentiate each other: the growth of convincing alternatives encourages attack on the old groups, while the loss of authority of the old structures facilitates development of the new.

I refer to the dam built on the Iato river: even though this "laboratory" is only a tiny part of the world, and still in its early stages, the sequence of events there provides a useful example.

A desperate population was dominated by the Mafia, strong through its political connections: there was no prospect of change. Together with the more enlightened people, we begin to seek possible remedies. The necessity and feasibility of building a large dam to irrigate the zone are established. Educational activity at the grass roots so that people understand what a dam is. Pressure, by a few at first, then growing ever wider and more continual, until the dam is started. The workers on the dam site form a trade union: jobs are no longer got through the Mafia, which loses prestige. Local *mafiosi* are publicly denounced; their relationship with the two powerful politicians from the area is likewise denounced; and two politicians are dropped from the Italian Government. Construction work is speeded up. Creation of the first (though still rudimentary) centers for promotion of a democratic irrigation syndicate to ensure non-Mafia water supply. Co-operatives are formed. In the neighboring Belice valley, pressure has begun for the construction of another, bigger dam; communal and intercommunal centers for organic planning are formed, and meanwhile another center is growing up at which people will learn the techniques of planned development with active involvement of the whole population.

Excerpt from Newsletter

It may be as well, then, to sum up our aims here, even at the risk of boring some of our more intimate friends, so as to make our position quite clear to the others. We feel we must:

—*disown violence,* above all in an area where thousands of persons have been murdered, 520 by the Mafia alone, since the war, and where violence is the only accepted law. We look upon violence, in all its forms, as a temptation to be resisted, as a festering evil;
—*disown falsehood,* another source of turbulence, especially in an area where the truth is rarely to be come by;
—*disown opportunism* of any sort;
—*disown fanaticism and dogmatism*—this is all the more necessary in an area where people are often ignorant of the very existence of the outside world, or of other ways of life, in an area where not even the most elementary organization exists for obtaining and analyzing data;
—*disown waste,* above all waste of human life.

Little by little, as we have been able to experiment for ourselves and discuss our problems with our friends, we have come to a clearer idea of our aims. They are these—we must:

—*work assiduously and eschew violence* for a new reality based on our sacrifice, in full awareness that if it sometimes becomes necessary to struggle to achieve our aims, our methods must be without reproach, since the end cannot be disassociated from the means, and in the knowledge that our every action has its inevitable consequences;
—*work in conformity with the truth,* while recognizing, at the same time, how difficult it can be to know what to do for the best;
—*open our hearts to the highest moral values,* wherever they may lie, so that the individual may have the opportunity of choosing his right road, so that the correct lessons may be learned from the most varied experiences;
—*work in accordance with a plan of education and reform,* which, while taking into account the complexity of life, shall bring into focus the objectives of the various groups of society and weld them into one harmonious, all-embracing order, so that, by bringing pressure to bear from within both on the quality and structure of society, one may seek to enhance the value of all men and all things.

The more perfect the methods, the more perfect the results; but nothing is perfect that has not the creation of life as its object.

OTHER WORKS BY DANILO DOLCI

A New World in the Making (New York: Monthly Review Press, 1965).
Poverty in Sicily (Harmondsworth, England: Penguin Books, 1966).
The Man Who Plays Alone (New York: Pantheon Books, 1968).
Report from Palermo (New York: Orion Press, 1959).

12 *Desiderius Erasmus*

*The man who symbolized the Renaissance, Deside-
rius Erasmus was a humanist, a monk, and a priest.
He preached the contradiction of war and Christianity, and called for a return to a simpler, more pure
form of Christian faith. The excerpt below * was
taken from* The Complaint of Peace, *Erasmus' mas-
terful polemic against war and the selfish political
motivations that caused war.*

Our Father

"Our Father," says he; O hardened wretch!
can you call him Father, when you are
just going to cut your brother's throat? "Hallowed be thy name":
how can the name of God be more impiously unhallowed, than
by mutual bloody murder among you, his sons? "Thy kingdom
come": do you pray for the coming of his kingdom, while you are
endeavoring to establish an earthly despotism, by spilling the blood
of God's sons and subjects? "Thy will be done on earth as it is in
heaven": his will in heaven is for peace, but you are now meditat-
ing war. Dare you to say to your Father in heaven: "Give us this
day our daily bread," when you are going, the next minute perhaps, to burn up your brother's corn-fields, and had rather lose the
benefit of them yourself, than suffer him to enjoy them unmolested? With what face can you say, "Forgive us our trespasses as
we forgive them that trespass against us," when, so far from for-
giving your own brother, you are going, with all the haste you
can, to murder him in cold blood, for an alleged trespass that,
after all, is but imaginary? Do you presume to deprecate the danger

---

* Taken from the text of a rare English version of *Complaint of Peace*. It
is probably the 1802 reprint of the translation made by T. Paynell but
published anonymously.

60

of temptation, who, not without great danger to yourself, are doing all you can to force your brother into danger? Do you deserve to be delivered from evil, that is, from the evil being, to whose impulse you submit yourself, and by whose spirit you are now guided, in contriving the greatest possible evil to your brother?

OTHER WORKS BY DESIDERIUS ERASMUS

Complaint of Peace (New York: Garland Publishers, 1971).

Erasmus and His Age (Selected Letters ed. by Hans J. Hillebrand) (New York: Harper and Row, 1970).

Adages, Margaret Mann Phillips, ed. (London: Cambridge University Press, 1967).

Praise of Folly (Baltimore: Penguin Books, 1971).

13 *George Fox*

The Quakers have traditionally been known as a peace church, holding to the belief that war is contrary to the spirit of Christ. The Quakers (Society of Friends) were founded in 1650 by George Fox, whose own life and writings attested to that conviction.

The first selection,* a letter to Oliver Cromwell was written in 1654 after Fox was accused of plotting to take Cromwell's life. In this letter he affirms that his intentions toward Cromwell—or any other man —are not violent. In the second selection,* Fox explains why he cannot fight.

Letter to Oliver Cromwell

I (who am of the world called George ffox) doe deny the carrying or drawing of any carnall sword against any, or against thee Oliver Cromwell or any men in presence of the lord God I declare it (God is my wittnesse, by whom I am moved to give this forth for truthes sake, from him whom the world calls George ffox, who is the son of God) who is sent to stand A wittnesse against all violence and against all the workes of darkenesse, and to turn people from the darknesse to the light, and to bring them from the occasion of the warre, and from the occasion of the Magistrates sword, which is A terrorism to the evill doers which actes contrary to the light of the lord Jesus Christ, which is A praise to them that doe well, which is A protection to

* Reprinted from *The Pacifist Conscience,* Peter Mayer, ed. (New York: Holt, Rinehart and Winston, 1967).

them that doe well, and not the evill and such soldiers that are putt in that place no false accusers must bee, no violence must doe, but bee content with their wages, and that Magistrate beares not the sword in vaine, from under the occasion of that sword I doe seeke to bring people, my weapons are not carnall but spirituall, And my Kingdome is not of this world, therefore with the carnall weapon I doe not fight, but am from those things dead, from him who is not of the world, called of the world by the name George ffox, and this I am ready to seale with my blood, and this I am moved to give forth for the truthes sake, who A wittnesse stand against all unrighteousnesse and all ungodlynesse, who A sufferer is for the righteous seed sake, waiteing for the redemption of it, who A crowne that is mortal seeks not for, that fadeth away, but in the light dwells, which comprehends that Crowne, which light is the condemnation of all such; in which Light I witnesse the Crowne that is Immortall that fades not away, from him who to all your soulls is A friend, for establishing of righteousnesse and cleansing the Land of evill doers, and A witnesse against all wicked inventions of men and murderous plotts, which Answered shall be with the light in all your Consciences, which makes no Covenant with death, to which light in you all I speake, and am clear.

ff. G.

The Time of My Commitment

Now the time of my commitment to the house of correction being nearly ended, and there being many new soldiers raised, the commissioners would have made me captain over them, and the soldiers said they would have none but me. So the keeper of the house of correction was commanded to bring me before the commissioners and soldiers in the market-place; and there they offered me that preferment, as they called it, asking me, if I would not take up arms for the Commonwealth against Charles Stuart? I told them, I knew from whence all wars arose, even from lust, according to James' doctrine; and that I lived in the virtue of that life and power that took away the occasion of all wars. But they courted me to accept their offer, and thought I did but compliment them. But I told them, I was come into the covenant of peace, which was before wars and strife were. They said, they offered it in love and kindness to me, because of my virtue; and such like flattering words they used. But I told them, if that was their love and kindness, I trampled it under my feet. Then their rage got up, and they said, 'Take him away, jailer, and put him into the dungeon amongst the rogues and felons.' So I was had away and put into a lousy, stinking place, without any bed, amongst thirty felons, where I was kept almost half a year, unless it were at times; for they would sometimes let me walk in the garden, having a belief that I would not go away. Now when they had got me into Derby dungeon it was the belief and saying of the people that I should never come out; but I had faith in God, and believed I should be delivered in his time; for the Lord had said to me before, that I was not to be removed from the place yet, being set there for a service which he had for me to do. . . .

All that pretend to fight for Christ, are deceived; for his kingdom is not of this world, therefore his servants do not fight. Fighters are not of Christ's kingdom, but are without Christ's kingdom; his kingdom starts in peace and righteousness, but fighters are in the lust; and all that would destroy men's lives, are not of Christ's mind, who came to save men's lives. Christ's kingdom is not of this world; it is peaceable: and all that are in strife, are not of his kingdom. All that pretend to fight for the Gospel, are deceived; for the Gospel is the power of God, which was before the devil, or fall of man was; and the gospel of peace was before fighting was. Therefore they that pretend fighting, are ignorant of the Gospel; and all that talk of fighting for Sion, are in darkness; for Sion needs no such helpers. All such as profess themselves to be ministers of Christ, or Christians, and go about to beat down the whore with outward, carnal weapons, the flesh and the whore are got up in themselves, and they are in a blind zeal; for the whore is got up by the inward ravening from the Spirit of God; and the beating down thereof, must be by the inward stroke of the sword of the

Spirit within. All such as pretend Christ Jesus, and confess him, and yet run into the use of carnal weapons, wrestling with flesh and blood, throw away the spiritual weapons. They that would be wrestlers with flesh and blood, throw away Christ's doctrine; the flesh is got up in them, and they are weary of their sufferings. Such as would revenge themselves, are out of Christ's doctrine. Such as being stricken on one cheek, would not turn the other, are out of Christ's doctrine: and such as do not love one another, nor love enemies, are out of Christ's doctrine.

RELATED READING BY GEORGE FOX

Journal (London: University of Cambridge Press, 1952).

14 *Mahatma Gandhi*

The prophet of 20th-century non-violence, Gandhi was to the Indian people a spiritual leader, a political realist, and a charismatic personal leader. His life view is deeply part of the religious and philosophical teachings of Hinduism and the ethics of Christianity. His writings and his life attest to his belief in the power of truth, the redemptive power of suffering, and the total equality of all men.

All of the excerpts that follow are from Gandhi's work, Non-Violent Resistance.*

Love

I accept the interpretation of *ahimsa,* namely, that it is not merely a negative state of harmlessness but it is a positive state of love, of doing good even to the evil-doer. But it does not mean helping the evil-doer to continue the wrong or tolerating it by passive acquiescence. On the contrary, love, the active state of *ahimsa,* requires you to resist the wrong-doer by dissociating yourself from him even though it may offend him or injure him physically. Thus if my son lives a life of shame, I may not help him to do so by continuing to support him; on the contrary, my love for him requires me to withdraw all support from him although it may mean even his death. And the same love imposes on me the obligation of welcoming him to my bosom when he repents. But I may not by physical force compel my son to become good. That in my opinion is the moral of the story of the Prodigal Son.

Non-cooperation is not a passive state; it is an intensely active

* Reprinted with the permission of the Navajivan Trust, Ahmedabad, India.

state—more active than physical resistance or violence. Passive resistance is a misnomer. Non-cooperation in the sense used by me must be non-violent and, therefore, neither punitive nor vindictive nor based on malice, ill-will or hatred. It follows therefore that it would be sin for me to serve General Dyer and cooperate with him to shoot innocent men. But it will be an exercise of forgiveness or love for me to nurse him back to life, if he was suffering from a physical malady. I would cooperate a thousand times with this Government to wean it from its career of crime, but I will not for a single moment cooperate with it to continue that career. And I would be guilty of wrong-doing if I retained a title from it or "a service under it or supported its law courts or schools." Better for me a beggar's bowl than the richest possession from hands stained with the blood of the innocents of Jalianwala. Better by far a warrant of imprisonment than honeyed words from those who have wantonly wounded the religious sentiment of my seventy million brothers.

My Faith

Non-cooperation and civil disobedience are but different branches of the same tree called Satyagraha. It is my *Kalpadruma*—my *Jam-i-Jam*—the Universal Provider. Satyagraha is search for Truth; and God is Truth. *Ahimsa* or non-violence is the light that reveals that Truth to me. Swaraj for me is part of that Truth. This Satyagraha did not fail me in South Africa, Kheda, or Champaran and in a host of other cases I could mention. It excludes all violence or hate. Therefore, I cannot and will not hate Englishmen. Nor will I bear their yoke. I must fight unto death the unholy attempt to impose British methods and British institutions on India. But I combat the attempt with non-violence. I believe in the capacity of India to offer non-violent battle to the English rulers. The experiment has not failed. It has succeeded, but not to the extent we had hoped and desired. I do not despair. On the contrary, I believe that India will come to her own in the near future, and that only through Satyagraha. The proposed suspension is part of the experiment. Non-cooperation need never be resumed if the program sketched by me can be fulfilled. Non-violent non-cooperation in some form or other, whether through the Congress or without it, will be resumed if the program fails. I have repeatedly stated that Satyagraha never fails and that one perfect Satyagrahi is enough to vindicate Truth. Let us all strive to be perfect Satyagrahis. The striving does not require any quality unattainable by the lowliest among us. For Satyagraha is an attribute of the spirit within. It is latent in every one of us. Like Swaraj it is our birthright. Let us know it.

Religious Satyagraha

Mixing up of motives is damaging in any species of Satyagraha, but in religious Satyagraha it is altogether inadmissible. It is fatal to use or allow religious Satyagraha to be used as a cloak or a device for advancing an ulterior political or mundane objective.

As with regard to the goal, so with the means: unadulterated purity is of the very essence in this species of Satyagraha. The leader in such a movement must be a man of deeply spiritual life, preferably a *brahmachari*—whether married or unmarried. He must be a believer in—as in fact everybody participating in such a movement must be—and practicer of the particular religious observance for which the movement is launched. The leader must be versed in the science of Satyagraha. Truth and *ahimsa* should shine through his speech. All his actions must be transparent through and through. Diplomacy and intrigue can have no place in his armory.

Absolute belief in *ahimsa* and in God is an indispensable condition in such Satyagraha.

In religious Satyagraha there can be no room for aggressiveness, demonstrativeness, show. Those who take part in it must have equal respect and regard for the religious convictions and susceptibilities of those who profess a different faith from theirs. The slightest narrowness in their outlook is likely to be reflected magnified multifold in the opponent.

Religious Satyagraha is, above all, a process of self-purification. It disdains mere numbers and external aids since these cannot add to the Satyagrahi's self-purification. Instead, it relies utterly on God who is the fountainhead of all strength. Religious Satyagraha, therefore, best succeeds under the leadership of a true man of God who will compel reverence and love even of the opponent by the purity of his life, the utter selflessness of his mission and the breadth of his outlook.

Non-Violence vs. Violence

I must resume the argument about the implications of the Rajkot step, where I left it the week before.

In theory, if there is sufficient non-violence developed in any single person, he should be able to discover the means of combating violence, no matter how widespread or severe, within his jurisdiction. I have repeatedly admitted my imperfections. I am no example of perfect *ahimsa*. I am evolving. Such *ahimsa* as has been developed in me has been found enough to cope with situations that have hitherto arisen. But today I feel helpless in the face of the surrounding violence. There was a penetrating article in the *Statesman* on my Rajkot statement. The editor had therein contended that the English had never taken our movement to be true Satyagraha, but being practical people they had allowed the myth to continue though they had known it to be a violent revolt. It was none the less so because the rebels had no arms. I have quoted the substance from memory. When I read the article, I felt the force of the argument. Though I had intended the movement to be pure non-violent resistance, as I look back upon the happenings of those days, there was undoubtedly violence among the resisters. I must own that had I been perfectly tuned to the music of *ahimsa,* I would have sensed the slightest departure from it and my sensitiveness would have rebelled against any discord in it.

It seems to me that the united action of the Hindus and the Muslims blinded me to the violence that was lurking in the breasts of many. The English who are trained diplomats and administrators are accustomed to the line of least resistance, and when they found that it was more profitable to conciliate a big organization than to crush it by extensive frightfulness, they yielded to the extent that they thought was necessary. It is, however, my conviction that our resistance was predominantly non-violent in action and will be accepted as such by the future historian. As a seeker of truth and non-violence, however, I must not be satisfied with mere action if it is not from the heart. I must declare from the housetops that the non-violence of those days fell far short of the non-violence I have so often defined.

Non-violent action without the cooperation of the heart and the head cannot produce the intended result. The failure of our imperfect *ahimsa* is visible to the naked eye. Look at the feud that is going on between Hindus and Muslims. Each is arming for the fight with the other. The violence that we had harbored in our breasts during the non-cooperation days is now recoiling upon ourselves. The violent energy that was generated among the masses, but was kept under check in the pursuit of a common objective, has now been let loose and is being used among and against ourselves.

The same phenomenon is discernible, though in a less crude manner, in the dissension among Congressmen themselves and the use of forcible methods that the Congress ministers are obliged to adopt in running the administrations under their charge.

This narrative clearly shows that the atmosphere is surcharged with violence. I hope it also shows that non-violent mass movement is an impossibility unless the atmosphere is radically changed. To blind one's eyes to the events happening around us is to court disaster. It has been suggested to me that I should declare that mass civil disobedience and all internal strife will cease, Hindus and Muslims will compose their differences, Congressmen will forget mutual jealousies and fights for power. My reading of the situation is wholly different. If any mass movement is undertaken at the present moment in the name of non-violence, it will resolve itself into violence largely unorganized and organized in some cases. It will bring discredit on the Congress, spell disaster for the Congress struggle for independence and bring ruin to many a home. This may be a wholly untrue picture born of my weakness. If so, unless I shed that weakness, I cannot lead a movement which requires great strength and resolution.

My Faith in Non-Violence

I have found that life persists in the midst of destruction and, therefore, there must be a higher law than that of destruction. Only under that law would a well-ordered society be intelligible and life worth living. And if that is the law of life, we have to work it out in daily life. Wherever there are jars, wherever you are confronted with an opponent, conquer him with love. In a crude manner I have worked it out in my life. That does not mean that all my difficulties are solved. I have found, however, that this law of love has answered as the law of destruction has never done. In India we have had an ocular demonstration of the operation of this law on the widest scale possible. I do not claim therefore that non-violence has necessarily penetrated the three hundred millions, but I do claim that it has penetrated deeper than any other message, and in an incredibly short time. We have not been all uniformly non-violent; and with the vast majority, non-violence has been a matter of policy. Even so, I want you to find out if the country has not made phenomenal progress under the protecting power of non-violence.

It takes a fairly strenuous course of training to attain to a mental state of non-violence. In daily life it has to be a course of discipline though one may not like it, like, for instance, the life of a soldier. But I agree that, unless there is a hearty cooperation of the mind, the mere outward observance will be simply a mask, harmful both to the man himself and to others. The perfect state is reached only when mind and body and speech are in proper coordination. But it is always a case of intense mental struggle. It is not that I am incapable of anger, for instance, but I succeed on almost all occasions to keep my feelings under control. Whatever may be the result, there is always in me a conscious struggle for following the law of non-violence deliberately and ceaselessly. Such a struggle leaves one stronger for it. Non-violence is a weapon of the strong. With the weak it might easily be hypocrisy. Fear and love are contradictory terms. Love is reckless in giving away, oblivious as to what it gets in return. Love wrestles with the world as with the self and ultimately gains mastery over all other feelings. My daily experience, as of those who are working with me, is that every problem lends itself to solution if we are determined to make the law of truth and non-violence the law of life. For truth and non-violence are, to me, faces of the same coin.

The law of love will work, just as the law of gravitation will work, whether we accept it or not. Just as a scientist will work wonders out of various applications of the law of nature, even so a man who applies the law of love with scientific precision can work greater wonders. For the force of non-violence is infinitely more wonderful and subtle than the material forces of nature, like, for instance, electricity. The men who discovered for us the law of love were greater scientists than any of our modern scientists. Only our explorations have not gone far enough and so it is not possible for everyone to see all its workings. Such, at any rate, is the hallucination, if it is one, under which I am laboring. The more I work at this law the more I feel the delight in life, the delight in the scheme of this universe. It gives me a peace and a meaning of the mysteries of nature that I have no power to describe.

OTHER WORKS BY MAHATMA GANDHI

Non-Violence in Peace and War (Ahmedabad, India: Navajivan Press, 1944-49).

Autobiography: My Experiments With Truth (Boston: Beacon Press, 1957).

Non-Violent Resistance (New York: Schocken Books, 1961).

All Men Are Brothers (Ahmedabad, India: Navajivan Press, 1960).

15 William Lloyd Garrison

A major figure in American non-violent history,
William Lloyd Garrison was instrumental in getting
the abolitionists to adopt the creed of non-violence.
Garrison called for an abolition of capital punishment, abstention from politics and abolition of all
war, as well as the emancipation of the slaves. In
1838 he joined with Adin Ballou to found the New
England Non-Resistance Society. The "Declaration
of Sentiments" * which appears below was adopted
by the American Peace Convention held in Boston in
1838.

Declaration of Sentiments, 1838

Assembled in Convention, from various
sections of the American Union, for the
promotion of peace on earth and good will among men, we, the
undersigned, regard it as due to ourselves, to the cause which we
love, to the country in which we live, and to the world, to publish
a Declaration, expressive of the principles we cherish, the purposes
we aim to accomplish, and the measures we shall adopt to carry
forward the work of peaceful and universal reformation.

We cannot acknowledge allegiance to any human government;
neither can we oppose any such government, by a resort of physical force. We recognize but one King and Lawgiver, one Judge
and Ruler of mankind. We are bound by the laws of a kingdom
which is not of this world; the subjects of which are forbidden to
fight; in which Mercy and Truth are met together, and Righteous-

* Reprinted from *Non-Violence in America: A Documentary History*,
Staughton Lynd, ed. (New York: The Bobbs-Merrill Company, Inc., 1966).

ness and Peace have kissed each other; which has no state lines, no national partitions, no geographical boundaries; in which there is no distinction or rank, or division of caste, or inequality of sex; the officers of which are Peace, its exactors Righteousness, its walls Salvation, and its gates Praise; and which is destined to break in pieces and consume all other kingdoms.

Our country is the world, our countrymen are all mankind. We love the land of our nativity, only as we love all other lands. The interests, rights, and liberties of American citizens are no more dear to us than are those of the whole human race. Hence, we can allow no appeal to patriotism, to revenge any national insult or injury. The Prince of Peace, under whose stainless banner we rally, came not to destroy, but to save, even the worst of enemies. He has left us an example, that we should follow his steps. "God commandeth his love toward us, in that while we were yet sinners, Christ died for us."

We conceive that if a nation has no right to defend itself against foreign enemies, or to punish its invaders, no individual possesses that right in his own case. The unit cannot be of greater importance than the aggregate. If one man may take life, to obtain or defend his rights, the same license must necessarily be granted to communities, states, and nations. If he may use a dagger or a pistol, they may employ cannon, bomb-shells, land and naval forces. The means of self-preservation must be in proportion to the magnitude of interests at stake, and the number of lives exposed to destruction. But if a rapacious and blood-thirsty soldiery, thronging these shores from abroad, with intent to commit rapine and destroy life, may not be resisted by the people or magistracy, then ought no resistance to be offered to domestic troublers of the public peace, or of private security. No obligation can rest upon Americans to regard foreigners as more sacred in their persons than themselves, or to give them a monopoly of wrong-doing with impunity.

The dogma that all the governments of the world are approvingly ordained of God, and that the powers that be in the United States, in Russia, in Turkey, are in accordance with His will, is not less absurd than impious. It makes the impartial Author of human freedom and equality, unequal and tyrannical. It cannot be affirmed that the powers that be, in any nation, are actuated by the spirit, or guided by the example of Christ, in the treatment of enemies; therefore, they cannot be agreeable to the will of God; and, therefore, their overthrow, by a spiritual regeneration of their subjects, is inevitable.

We register our testimony, not only against all wars, whether offensive or defensive, but all preparations for war; against every naval ship, every arsenal, every fortification; against the militia system and a standing army; against all military chieftains and soldiers; against all monuments commemorative of victory over a foreign foe, all trophies won in battle, all celebrations in honor of military or naval exploits; against all appropriations for the defense of a nation by force and arms on the part of any legislative body; against every edict of government, requiring of its subjects military service. Hence, we deem it unlawful to bear arms, or to hold a military office.

As every human government is upheld by physical strength, and its laws are enforced virtually at the point of the bayonet, we cannot hold any office which imposes upon its incumbent the obligation to do right, on pain of imprisonment or death. We therefore voluntarily exclude ourselves from every legislative and judicial body, and repudiate all human politics, worldly honors, and stations of authority. If *we* cannot occupy a seat in the legislature, or on the bench, neither can we elect *others* to act as our substitutes in any such capacity.

It follows that we cannot sue any man at law, to compel him by force to restore any thing which he may have wrongfully taken from us or others; but, if he has seized our coat, we shall surrender up our cloak, rather than subject him to punishment.

We believe that the penal code of the old covenant, an eye for an eye, and a tooth for a tooth, has been abrogated by Jesus Christ; and that, under the new covenant, the forgiveness instead of the punishment of enemies has been enjoined upon all his disciples, in all cases whatsoever. To extort money from enemies, or set them upon a pillory, or cast them into prison, or hang them upon a gallows, is obviously not to forgive, but to take retribution. "Vengeance is mine—I will repay, saith the Lord."

The history of mankind is crowded with evidences, proving that physical coercion is not adapted to moral regeneration; that the sinful disposition of man can be subdued only by love; that evil can be exterminated from the earth only by goodness; that it is not safe to rely upon an arm of flesh, upon man, whose breath is in his nostrils, to preserve us from harm; that there is great security in being gentle, harmless, long-suffering, and abundant in mercy; that it is only the meek who shall inherit the earth, for the violent, who resort to the sword, shall perish with the sword. Hence, as a measure of sound policy, of safety to property, life, and liberty, of public quietude and private enjoyment, as well as on the ground of allegiance to Him who is King of kings, and Lord of lords, we cordially adopt the non-resistance principle, being confident that it provides for all possible consequences, will ensure all things needful to us, is armed with omnipotent power, and must ultimately triumph over every assailing force.

We advocate no jacobinal doctrines. The spirit of jacobinism is the spirit of retaliation, violence and murder. It neither fears God, nor regards man. We would be filled with the spirit of Christ. If we abide by our principles, it is impossible for us to be disorderly, or plot treason, or participate in any evil work: we shall submit to every ordinance of man, for the Lord's sake; obey all the requirements of government, except such as we deem contrary to the commands of the Gospel; and in no wise resist the operation of law, except by meekly submitting to the penalty of disobedience.

But, while we shall adhere to the doctrines of non-resistance and passive submission to enemies, we purpose, in a moral and spiritual sense, to speak and act boldly in the cause of God; to assail iniquity in high places and in low places; to apply our principles to all existing civil, political, legal, and ecclesiastical institutions; and to hasten the time when the kingdoms of this world shall become the kingdoms of our Lord and of his Christ, and he shall reign forever.

It appears to us a self-evident truth that, whatever the Gospel is designed to destroy at any period of the world, being contrary to it, ought now to be abandoned. If, then, the time is predicted when swords shall be beaten into plough-shares, and spears into pruning-hooks, and men shall not learn the art of war any more, it follows that all who manufacture, sell, or wield those deadly weapons, do thus array themselves against the peaceful dominion of the Son of God on earth.

Having thus briefly, but frankly, stated our principles and purposes, we proceed to specify the measures we propose to adopt, in carrying our object into effect.

We expect to prevail through the foolishness of preaching— striving to commend ourselves unto every man's conscience, in the sight of God. From the press, we shall promulgate our sentiments as widely as practicable. We shall endeavor to secure the cooperation of all persons, of whatever name or sect. The triumphant progress of the cause of Temperance and of Abolition in our land, through the instrumentality of benevolent and voluntary associations, encourages us to combine our own means and efforts for the promotion of a still greater cause. Hence we shall employ lecturers, circulate tracts and publications, form societies, and petition our state and national governments in relation to the subject of Universal Peace. It will be our leading object to devise ways and means for effecting a radical change in the views, feelings and practices of society respecting the sinfulness of war, and the treatment of enemies.

In entering upon the great work before us, we are not unmindful that, in its prosecution, we may be called to test our sincerity, even as in a fiery ordeal. It may subject us to insult, outrage, suffering, yea, even death itself. We anticipate no small amount of misconception, misrepresentation, calumny. Tumults may arise against us. The ungodly and violent, the proud and pharisaical, the ambitious and tyrannical, principalities and powers, and spiritual wickedness in high places, may combine to crush us. So they treated the Messiah, whose example we are humbly striving to imitate. If we suffer with him, we know that we shall reign with him. We shall not be afraid of their terror, nor be troubled. Our confidence is in the Lord Almighty, not in man. Having withdrawn from human protection, what can sustain us but that faith which overcomes the world? We shall not think it strange concerning the fiery trial which is to try us, as though some strange thing had happened unto us; but rejoice, inasmuch as we are partakers of Christ's sufferings. Wherefore, we commit the keeping of our souls to God, in well-doing, as unto a faithful Creator. "For everyone that forsakes houses, or brethren, or sisters, or father, or mother, or wife, or children, or lands, for Christ's sake, shall receive an hundred fold, and shall inherit everlasting life."

Firmly relying upon the certain and universal triumph of the sentiments contained in this Declaration, however formidable may be the opposition arrayed against them, in solemn testimony of our faith in their divine origin, we hereby afix our signatures to it, commending it to the reason and conscience of mankind, giving ourselves no anxiety as to what may befall us, and resolving, in the strength of the Lord God, calmly and meekly to abide the issue.

OTHER RELATED WORKS

The Letters of William Lloyd Garrison, Walter Merrill, ed. (Cambridge, Mass.: Harvard University Press, 1971).

William Lloyd Garrison, George Frederickson, ed. (Englewood Cliffs, N.J.: Prentice-Hall, 1968).

William Lloyd Garrison on Non-Resistance by Fannt Garrison Villard (New York: Nation Press Printing Co., 1924).

16 *Hildegaard Goss-Mayr*

An Austrian by birth, Hildegaard Goss-Mayr and her husband, Jean Goss, have worked extensively in South and Latin America, as well as in Europe, as field secretaries for the International Fellowship of Reconciliation. She writes out of deep experience and commitment to the principles of non-violence. The following selection is a talk given at CIDOC in August 1970.

Active Non-Violence

First of all I should like to present myself and my husband. We work together, and therefore if I speak of "us," it is always the two of us.

Jean and I have been secretaries of the International Fellowship of Reconciliation, which is an ecumenical peace movement, for a number of years. Our work, in particular during the time of the cold war, has been in East-West relations in Europe. We tried to establish a dialogue between Christians and non-Christians at the time when it was still very difficult to get through the "Iron Curtain." Later on we built up a kind of peace lobby at the Vatican Council and we tried to push the bishops and theologians of the Catholic Church—we are Catholic ourselves—to develop a dynamic theology of peace. We Christians have not really brought forth the peace-making and transforming forces that are in the Gospel. There we met a number of Latin American bishops, among them Dom Helder Camara. They invited us to come to Latin America to study the situation and perhaps, if it seemed possible, to begin training groups in non-violent resistance against social and economic injustices and other forms of exploitation. This has been our work in Brazil in 1964/1965 and later on in other parts of Latin America.

Now I should like to ask you not to take the expression *non-violence* in a negative sense. It is a very negative expression for something which is highly active, aggressive and strong; which is a force. We regret that we have not found a better word to express this type of action. I hope we will not limit ourselves to discuss this term but try to get the sense, the real meaning for which it stands.

There are in man three possibilities to react against injustice:

1. Once you have become aware of an injustice you can remain passive. This is the first and I think the most common attitude. Probably each one of us has had this experience in his own life. We have accepted passively many injustices, many things that we considered wrong. This is the most negative attitude that man can take.

2. The second is the traditional way of reacting against injustice, the way that has been taken in history in general, that is, to react against injustice, aggression and other forms of evil with the same means. We could say to oppose the institutional forms of violence with counter-violence in the effort to overcome existing injustices. This means to resort to the same means with which the established forces are operating. By doing this, we remain, however, within the system, that is to say, we accept to remain within the vicious circle of violence and counter-violence which necessarily creates new forms of violence, even if we succeed to overcome certain injustices through the application of violence. It must be made very clear that the means are linked to the aim. That is to say, the use of violence in the effort to overcome injustice necessarily creates new forms of suppression and exploitation. Acting in this way one remains within the vicious circle of arms' trade, money speculation, verbal promises etc., and the mass of the people continue to suffer exploitation and injustice. There has been, perhaps more in our time than before, more serious research concerning a new way of fighting against injustice by using means that do not include hatred, violence, etc.

3. Perhaps this third way of reacting against an injustice could be explained through a very simple example. I have two children. If, for instance, my boy, who is ten and by nature violent, has done something wrong and if I use the same aggressive means as he does, we shall just hurt each other. He does not improve and I must tell

myself: "Well, you have not done anything to overcome the evil." On the contrary, if one really wanted to solve the problem, a teacher or parent would explain to the young person why his way of acting is wrong and help him to direct his forces toward positive tasks. That is to say, you dialogue, you begin to use certain methods and techniques in order to solve the conflict. In this process neither of us is diminished; on the contrary, he advances and I begin to understand him better and to learn about what he has to contribute. This force is the force of intelligence but also the force of truth, of love and justice that has been brought into play in this effort of solving a problem. This is the type of strength which is at the core of non-violent action.

There are always two aspects in this form of action which are inseparable. If they are separated, we can no longer speak of an authentic non-violent action. These two aspects are: (1) a specific view of man, a certain attitude toward men and society, and (2) certain techniques and methods that correspond to this attitude and that incarnate this force in a given conflict. This technique and this view go together and cannot be separated.

A New Attitude Toward Man

Now, which attitude toward life, toward man does it imply? First of all, an *absolute respect* of man, of his whole life, in body and spirit. Secondly, the conviction that *man is man*. We very often do not believe anymore that man is man, but we put a label, we say he is a communist, he is a conservative, he is black, he is white, and we do not see anymore the man behind the ideology, the religion or the race which he presents.

Those who work with this power of non-violence believe that *every man has a conscience*. This conscience may be uneducated, underdeveloped; it may, by tradition, be deformed; but it is there —and if work is done, this conscience can be awakened, it can be challenged, it can be reached. I think this is truly an aspect of hope; if we cannot believe anymore that man is man, in this sense, in the final analysis, there is then no other way than to use the old traditional forms of violence in trying to solve our problems. This implies that *man must never be identified with evil*. As long as we identify him with evil we sacrifice him to an ideology. On the contrary the task of the non-violent action is *to fight the injustice and to liberate men,* those who suffer the injustice as well as those who are responsible for it. This therefore is a very constructive, positive and active form of living.

There are different ways of reaching this view. It may be through a humanistic attitude, it may be through religion, Buddhism, Hinduism or Christianity. Personally I believe that the essential point of the Christian faith is precisely this aspect. In this lies the revolutionary aspect of our faith. We are challenged, we are asked to reply in a radically new way to evil. It is our specific task to introduce this new way of fighting injustice into the historical situation that we are experiencing. For Christ has shown us a new view of man. Going beyond the Old Testament attitude of considering as one's "neighbors" only those of one's own clan, that is to say, the Jewish people, he teaches that *every human being* without exception, even the enemy, is in a very realistic sense *our neighbor*. This implies that we react to those who stand against us in a radically new way, a way that refuses all means that diminish, violate or destroy them, but which, on the contrary, tries to overcome the evil that separates us. Christ has not only taught this, he has lived it and furthermore has shown some techniques of how to live that force in a specific historical situation. He attacked the status quo of his time, those who betrayed men and were the privileged. He attacked the established Church of his time. He attacked the conscience of its representatives throughout the three years of his public life so strongly that they reacted *in the traditional way with violence* against him and crucified him. He was not crucified because he did nothing, but exactly because he attacked the injustice of his time in a very clear and precise way and because he spoke the truth. But he always respected men. Neither did he join the established groups of his time nor the guerrilla who operated in Israel, and who wanted to liberate the country from the Roman occupation. He showed a new way of fighting evil and he was willing to accept the consequences of his action.

This is something we must bear in mind: The moment we attack an injustice, we must be prepared and willing to accept the sacrifices and the suffering that necessarily will result from our attack. For those whose conscience is attacked will as a first reaction use violence against us. This may be the cross for some of those engaged in a non-violent action.

Techniques of Non-Violent Action

I think it has already become clear that this kind of action has nothing to do with a sentimental form of love or of being nice. It is a strategy, it is a way to act, it is a struggle that has to be carried on to the last consequences. If it remains only a single, sporadic action it will not succeed. This implies that non-violent workers have to undergo *training*—just as a soldier is trained for violent combat.

During recent years research on non-violent alternatives has been taken up on various scientific levels, as for instance political science, sociology, education, psychology, etc., in various Peace Research Institutes. Only very recently, however, non-violent action is being given more and serious attention and an effort is made to relate it to the various levels of human life. But we are still only at the very beginning and nobody can propose a complete and perfect strategy. There is no universal model of action. Non-violent strategy has to be adapted to the need, to the particular situation and problem that is involved. Thus Gandhi's or Martin Luther King's methods cannot simply be transferred to the Latin American scene. From their strategies we can learn certain basic principles and develop and apply them in an adequate way to given conditions.

I should like to add that it is significant that these methods, so far, have mainly been used by the poor; I think non-violence is essentially an arm of the poor, a force of liberation for them. Not only do they have no access to the arms of the rich, they often passively accept injustice because they are unaware of the power of resistance that lies within them because they are human beings. It is an essential task to make them aware of this force and train them to apply it. Most of the non-violent actions that have been realized in Latin America so far have been carried out by the very

poor people, by industrial workers and campesinos, on the planta-
tions or in the barrios of the cities.

A Few Basic Principles of Non-Violent Strategy

1. *Analysis.* One has to be aware of the injustice in order to be
able to fight it. You have to analyze very well the situation, not
only its local aspect but the whole context in which it occurs; for
instance, if you work for economic and social justice in Latin
America, you must make the complete analysis and see how it is
linked to the economic and military policy of the rich countries.

2. *Form action groups and train leadership.* If there is no local
leadership, an action will not succeed; I think so far this has been
one of the weak points in non-violent action.

3. *Then select a limited and well-defined first project.* It must be
at the level where the people with whom you work can understand
it and where they are capable to solve it with their small forces.
It is very important, in particular if you work with poor people for
whom it may be the first time that they act, that this action makes
them aware of their own strength. I remember working in Medellín,
Colombia, with a group in a barrio. There were about 5,000 people
who had occupied land on a steep hill above the city. They had
neither water nor electricity, canalization or schools. Many were
unemployed. A priest who came to live with them developed leadership and tried to stimulate initiatives among the people to change
their dismal conditions. With his help a seminar on non-violent
action was organized in which did participate not only representatives of the barrio but also students, teachers, social workers,
intellectuals, priests, etc. It was for them, who knew poverty only
from statistics, a challenging experience to live in the mud of the
barrio. It helped to bridge the gap between the poor and the educated and to make them understand the necessity of working
together for justice for all. The objective was, after having trans-
mitted the basic facts about non-violence and its methods of action,
and after having analyzed their situation, to make the poor people
themselves decide upon their first project and to outline their plan
of action. They decided that their most urgent problem was water:
they learned how to negotiate, how to bring their problem before

the mind of the responsible people—who live far from the reality of the poor—how to build up their forces with the help of conscious and educated people and to win the support of a growing section of the population. They learned to use their imagination and to try out their human, moral and political power in this first project. They did win and helped themselves to build their water pipes. From there they went on to electricity, schooling, labor, etc. They had experienced the power of man to work for change.

4. *Expansion to the international level.* Then, once you act against one injustice, you see how it is linked to others, nationally and internationally. Therefore in the future the strategy must be to join actions in Africa, Asia or Latin America where people are working, for instance for land reform or where they are suffering particularly from the exploitation by certain international companies or from certain economic policies of the industrialized countries, with efforts in Europe and in the United States which are directed at changing these injustices. This means to put pressure on our political, economic and cultural groups, and upon our Churches in order to finally transform this system of exploitation. We are facing a task that concerns humanity as such. It is impossible for the developing countries to bring about the necessary changes unless in the rich countries as well the change of our economic, political and military system is obtained.

5. *Progression of means.* Direct action, strike, boycott, and immobilization are some of the heavier arms of non-violent action. Again, these actions must be adapted to the situation in which the struggle is taking place. However, after serious reflection and preparation much more is possible in the way of action than we imagine in general, even under most difficult circumstances. The most instructive example of recent times is that of the Tcheque people who did succeed in organizing the whole nation in a boycott against the invading Soviet troops. It showed what a whole nation is able to do if her people are very deeply concerned about certain injustices and are willing to accept the consequences of their collective action.

17 James Groppi

Father James Groppi is an activist priest from Milwaukee, and has long been involved in the struggle for human rights. At times his activism has been a source of embarrassment to his Church, but he has served as an inspiration and vocal presence to many young people involved in the problems of contemporary America. The selection below * deals with the subtle forms violence often takes.

Violence

Violence is many things. It's watching little black children go to bed at night wondering whether or not the rats will come through the wall and bite them.

It's sitting in the house for two weeks with overcoats on and wrapped in blankets trying to keep warm.

Violence is watching the kids across the street walk out of the house without any shoes on.

It's knowing they're wondering whether they'll get a next meal.

Courts

I went to court. The two D.A.'s were both white. The judge was white. There were eleven white jurors, and one black man who had a habit of nodding his head. I knew where I stood.

And this is how a black man feels.

The same judge who gave me a six months stay of sentence, two years probation and a $500 fine, had previously sentenced a landlord who owns 16 slum houses. One house had 27 building code

* Reprinted from *Motive* Magazine, February 1969, Volume XXIX, Number 5.

violations; another had 34. That same judge gave the landlord a stay of sentence and fined him $1 each on 12 of the properties.

The average fine paid in Milwaukee on building code violations is $35, including court costs. Draft protestors were recently placed under $25,000 bond. But two white men recently went before the same judge and were released on $2,500 bond. They had ridden through the black community, stuck a .22 rifle out of the window, and killed a black woman. A black Vietnam veteran was arrested as a suspect in a burglary—$25,000 bond. Two Klansmen bombed the Milwaukee NAACP office and were out on $2,500 bond.

This is the kind of judicial system we live under. This is the one the black man sees.

The Poor Pay More

I was sitting on the rectory steps. Some of the brothers and sisters came from Third Street carrying clothing, furniture, and a few small items. "Hi, Father Groppi. Black Power!" they called, pointing to their loot. I said, "Be careful. Don't get caught."

That surprises you. But maybe you don't know much about gyp merchants. You go in a store and there are no prices on the merchandise. Or old stuff is sold for new. Or they sell you a $3 pair of shoes for $25.

Go read *The Poor Pay More*. The author sent a white man into a Harlem store to buy a TV set. The charge was $129. A Puerto Rican woman who followed paid $139. The black woman who came next paid $200.

That's stealing. And there's no difference between that kind of thievery and the man who busts the window and grabs the loot. Maybe he figures he's got it coming. He's probably paid for it five times over already.

Robbery? I call it restitution.

Fair Housing

We marched for fair housing. They asked, "Why are you working on a fair housing bill? Do black people want to live with white people?" I said, "I don't know." We'll never know until white people's intransigent attitude toward integration, and toward equality, is changed.

But the black man needs territorial expansion. If all the white people want to move to the suburbs, fine. But we want to live in fine communities too.

We marched twice on the south side of Milwaukee and nearly got killed by whites. I asked for the protection of the National Guard, but the Mayor said he couldn't call them out. "Good hardworking people live out there," he said.

I don't know how good they were, but they were certainly hardworking. They hit us with everything they could throw. They called us black bastards. And then violence broke out on the north side. The Mayor called out the National Guard and put the entire city under a curfew . . . and issued a proclamation. He didn't want us to demonstrate, he didn't want us to march, he didn't want us to use civil disobedience. He said it led to violence.

What are we supposed to do? Submit to this kind of system?

BOOK ABOUT JAMES GROPPI

Frank A. Aukofer, *City With a Chance* (Milwaukee: Bruce, 1968).

18 *Thich Nhat Hanh*

A Vietnamese poet and scholar, Thich Nhat Hanh refuses to be identified with any of the factions in Vietnam, with the exception of the poor and the young. He is one of the major voices urging peace and social reconstruction in Vietnam, as the following poem illustrates. The second selection * deals with the non-violent struggle for peace in Vietnam.

Condemnation

Listen to this:
Yesterday six Vietcong came through my village.
Because of this my village was bombed—completely destroyed.
Every soul was killed.
When I come back to my village now, the day after,
There is nothing to see but clouds of dust and the river, still flowing.
The pagoda has neither roof nor altar.
Only the foundations of houses are left.
The bamboo thickets are burned away.

Here in the presence of the undisturbed stars,
In the invisible presence of all the people still alive on earth,
Let me raise my voice to denounce this filthy way,
This murder of brothers by brothers!
I have a question: Who pushed us into this killing of one another?

Whoever is listening, be my witness!
I cannot accept this war,
I never could, I never shall.
I have to say this a thousand times before I am killed.

I feel I am like a bird which dies for the sake of its mate,

* Reprinted from Fellowship Magazine, January 1970.

Dripping blood from its broken beak, and crying out:
Beware! Turn around and face your real enemies—
Ambition, violence, hatred, greed.

Men cannot be our enemies—even men called "Vietcong"!
If we kill men, what brothers will we have left?
With whom shall we live then?

Love in Action

The Vietnamese people are suffering a period of agony unprecedented in our history. Along with the struggle for national independence, a parallel struggle is going on between two conflicting ideologies. At the heart of both, the intervening hands of foreign powers can be clearly seen.

The socialist bloc hopes to extend the zone of Communist influence. The capitalist bloc supports Vietnamese who call themselves "anti-Communist" with the intention of extending the zone of capitalist influence. The imperialistic powers, in one way or another, have penetrated deeply into the Vietnamese conflict.

The nature of the Vietnamese war is not that simple, however. In all aspects of their lives the Vietnamese have resisted becoming victims of international conflicts. In the past this ability has prevented them from being assimilated by other powers; it has enabled them fully to manifest and develop their own characteristics, and to build a truly independent Vietnamese culture. When this terrible war is over, the Vietnamese will again have assimilated into their culture aspects of the cultures which are confronting each other in their land, but only those that fulfill Vietnamese needs. Vietnamese culture has always been able to retain its own native characteristics.

Long before the introduction of Buddhism into Vietnam, the Vietnamese had developed strong indigenous characteristics. Thus they were able to assimilate Buddhism and transform it into a Vietnamese Buddhism that became the cornerstone on which to build an independent culture. The Chinese discovered that bringing Chinese Buddhism into Vietnam did not help them conquer and assimilate the Vietnamese. Instead, it helped the Vietnamese to build the self-reliance and independence to resist invasion from the North. After liberation from Chinese domination the Vietnamese were more determined than ever to develop an independent culture.

The Humanist Influence of Buddhism

But the introduction of Buddhism into Vietnam at an early date greatly enhanced the development of Vietnamese culture. It contributed enormously to the advancement of art, education, social work and politics. During the 11th century its influence enabled the Vietnamese to establish a stable base for politics, economics and education, as an independent nation. Even more important, a genuinely humanist culture had been formed. Guided by the spirit of humanism taught by Buddhism, political and intellectual leaders were able to transform the rather barbarous ways of the early epochs into the compassionate and civilized culture of the Ly dynasty which prevailed for over two hundred years.

Buddhism has never tried to obstruct other cultural influences, nor has it tried to destroy other ideologies, whether Vietnamese or imported from the outside, whether Confucian, Taoist, Christian, Cao Dai, or Hoa Hao.

The aspirations for peace, the ability to assimilate, the patience and endurance of the Vietnamese people are all important factors where Buddhism and Vietnamese culture meet. While possessing hundreds of doctrinal and philosophical systems, Buddhism is not a structure of dogmas. Without a spirit of understanding and tolerance, Buddhism can no longer be itself. Hence, tremendous powers of assimilation and reconciliation are inherent in Buddhism, allowing it to adapt easily to local conditions, in any area, and to contribute to the building and enrichment of the local culture. The cult of ancestors in Vietnam, for example, has been accepted and assimilated by Buddhism.

In their relations with Catholics, Vietnamese Buddhists have been very patient. Although aware that Catholicism is an alien way of life to the Vietnamese, they have been applying the method of dialogue, thus encouraging and contributing to efforts to Vietnamize the Catholic community in Vietnam. This demands much time and effort, because since its introduction into Vietnam, Catholicism has firmly retained the modes of thinking and worship of the Western Church, and because attempts have been made by imperialistic and colonialist forces dominating the country to use the Catholic Church in Vietnam to further their own ends.

Vietnamese Resist Western Ways

As for the Communist movement, from the beginning Vietnamese Buddhists have been making inquiries in an effort to establish dialogue. Since the Buddhists are close to the resistance movement for independence, they have more opportunities than the Catholics to understand their Communist countrymen. Here, the Buddhist attitude is not antagonistic, but cautious. While they are aware of the anti-religious nature of Communism, as well as its dogmatic tendencies, the Buddhists also see the efforts of the Communists in the struggle for independence and social progress. That is why they keep the door for dialogue open wide.

Unlike other religions, Buddhism is not limited to those who call themselves Buddhists; it has penetrated into the very marrow of Vietnam. True to the Buddhist spirit, people in the North as well as the South have been striving to transcend all ideologies and doctrines. Thus, while there are still many dogmatic Communists, Communism in Vietnam is on the way to being Vietnamized. It entered Vietnam as a Western weapon to oppose Western colonialism, following the French occupation of Vietnam. When it was found to be effective in combatting colonialism, some Vietnamese embraced Communism in a fanatical way until it became, to them, more important than the values of traditional Vietnamese culture.

But suffering has helped us to see that we cannot rigidly apply Western thought to an analysis of Vietnamese problems. Americans failed in Vietnam because they came with knowledge obtained in Western schools and Western books to try to solve Vietnamese problems. Attempts to force Western democracy upon us ended up creating comical activities labeled "democratic ways of life." Communists, too, tried in a very unnatural and awkward way to fit the social, cultural and historical realities of Vietnam into Marxist patterns of thought. We have seen the effects of fanatical, dogmatic ideologies in the blood and fire of Vietnam. Fascism, Communism and anti-Communism have spread pain and suffering everywhere.

The struggle by the Buddhist community should be understood in the light of the struggle of the whole population for survival, for a progressive, humanist way of life, and above all, *to remain Vietnamese*. The means of struggle must not destroy the Vietnamese character. That is why the Buddhist community began its non-violent struggle in 1963. Each effort to achieve peace and harmony made by Vietnamese, whether Communist or Catholic, in the North or the South, is in harmony with the non-violent struggle by the Buddhists.

Non-Violence Is Not a Doctrine

There was a time when humanist and religious leaders in the West admired the non-violent struggle for Indian independence led by Gandhi. They analyzed it and tried to apply his principles. But by thinking in terms of "methods" and "techniques" they failed to see the essence of non-violent action and eventually many lost faith in its effectiveness.

The non-violent struggle in Vietnam did not begin with a theory but with an awareness of the suffering caused by violence. Because the situation of Vietnam is unique, Vietnamese Buddhists cannot imitate others. History demonstrates that non-violent action requires creativity, thorough understanding of the mentality of the people, and, above all, a resisting spiritual force. Organizational techniques are not sufficient for success.

In May, 1966, when the people of Hue and Danang learned that Marshal Ky was bringing tanks and troops from Saigon in American planes to suppress their movement, they brought their family altars into the streets to oppose the tanks. This action may be considered a tactic, but considered only as such, the deeper part of the action, and the very nature of the struggle, is missed. The family altars symbolized the spiritual force of the people and their traditional values directly challenging the foreign and anti-humanist forces in their midst.

The Nature of the Non-Violent Struggle

The nature of the struggle is not a doctrine to be materialized by a program of action; it is communication and love. Thus, its leaders must create and inspire love for the masses in the hearts of their people. They touch the people by altruistic acts born from their own love. When Nhat Chi Mai burned herself because she wanted to be a "torch in the dark night," she moved millions of Vietnamese. The force she engendered was the force of love for non-violent action.

We have witnessed tragic and heroic scenes of love: a monk seated calmly before advancing tanks; women and children raising bare hands against clubs and grenades; hunger strikes held in patience and silence. *Only love and sacrifice can engender love and sacrifice.* This chain reaction is essential to the non-violent struggle. Thich Tri Quang did not make strategy; he fasted 100 days. And everyone who passed by the Duy Tan clinic at that time had to hold his breath.

The usual way to generate force is to create anger, desire and fear. But these are dangerous sources of energy because they are blind, whereas the force of love springs from awareness, and does not destroy its own aims. Out of love and the willingness to act, strategies and tactics will be created naturally from the circumstances of the struggle. Thus, the problems of strategy and tactics are of secondary importance. They should be posed, but not at the beginning. Obviously, absolutely non-violent action cannot really exist. So the problem is not one of absolutes, but of the extent to which we can follow the principle of non-violence. Political means, for instance, can be non-violent. And in that respect, the warring parties in Vietnam have been applying non-violent means, along with violence. The problem is to find a way to avoid violence as far as possible.

The non-violent struggle for independence and peace in Vietnam has deep roots. From the mid-19th century on, Buddhist clergymen helped in the struggle to gain independence from France. Today they still have the trust and support they won from their followers along with knowledge gained. Their theory of the equilibrium of forces and the Program of the Buddhist Socialist Bloc indicate a sound understanding of the political situation in Vietnam and the world. The theory of the equilibrium of forces expresses the belief that peace in Vietnam can be achieved and safeguarded only through neutrality, a neutrality agreed upon and respected by all nations. The program demands reverence and respect for the lives of Vietnamese and the placing of Vietnam above any ideology. "Man is not our enemy" expresses our principle of action, and our struggle's purpose: the destruction of fanaticism and inhumanity, which are the real enemies of man. The non-violent struggle rejects fanatical Communism and fanatical anti-Communism. It stresses harmony, open-mindedness, humanism.

Humanists in the Midst of War

The Buddhist movement has worked for a humanist revolution in Vietnamese society. The Program of the Buddhist Socialist Bloc aims at a neutral Vietnam, friendly to all nations and ready to learn from all in order to enrich the Vietnamese way. Van Hanh University, founded by Buddhists, has started a Faculty of Political Science. The Buddhist School of Youth for Social Service trains workers for rural reconstruction. The Buddhist movement has encouraged others to engage in social service and has spurred on the formation of professional unions.

In the domain of the arts and of literature, there has been active participation in the movement for peace and reconciliation since 1963. There are anti-war writers, composers, poets and artists. Anti-war songs are sung in the streets and in classrooms. In spite of the danger, anti-war literature is widely circulated, even among army units. Many people have been arrested simply for possession of it.

The Buddhist movement has tried to ally itself with all religious and social forces working for peace and independence. Among these are progressive Cao-Dai, Hoa Hao and Catholics, who have joined the cause in increasing numbers. As the movement has grown, more and more of these have become friends of the Buddhists. The movement also tries to draw support from members of the National Liberation Front and people in the Saigon government who desire peace and are for the national culture. Many in both places support the movement. From its inception the Buddhist movement has tried to work with humanist and pacifist movements throughout the world, especially with the American anti-war movement. Where it could, the Overseas Vietnamese Buddhist Association has helped to create and maintain pressure to end the war. The Buddhist movement has also allied itself with the civil rights movement in the United States. At Chicago on June 1, 1966, during a joint press conference with a Buddhist monk, Rev. Dr. Martin Luther King declared, "Both the colored people struggling for civil rights in the United States and the Buddhists struggling for peace in Vietnam are bound to the cause of peace and social justice, and are determined to sacrifice themselves to achieve their goal."

Buddhists Die To Protest the War

As the war's brutality spread and grew, individual Buddhists were driven to protest through an act of supreme sacrifice: self-immolation. Such acts are not included in any program of action, for no one has the courage to arrange the ending of another's life by fire. When an individual declares his intention to do this, the Buddhist Church tries to dissuade him. At the same time, it is understood that a person who has come to such a decision has moved out beyond the church's authority. In Vietnam, members of the clergy, laymen, even young students have made this tragic, painful sacrifice for peace. Westerners often misunderstand, and see self-immolation as an act of violence. To the Vietnamese it is quite the opposite. By accepting extreme suffering, one lights the fires of compassion and awakens the hearts of the people, as Christ did. Among a number of Vietnamese who have immolated themselves for peace were Thich Quang Duc, a monk, and Nhat Chi Mai, a young girl student.

Another means—the one most often used by Gandhi to communicate with the people—has been fasting. Thousands of Vietnamese, both as individuals and in groups, have fasted to try to end the war. One fasts to pray, to purify one's heart and strengthen the will—or to arouse the latent awareness and compassion of the population. In 1966, Venerable Thich Tri Quang fasted for 100 days, deeply affecting the people of Vietnam.

There have been other painful sacrifices. In 1963, a girl student named Mai Tuyet An cut off her hand as a warning to the Diem regime, unleashing tremendous emotion among young people. In 1966, ten university students, Nhat Chi Mai among them, pledged to kill themselves to try to end the war, but the church forbade them. A year later, Nhat Chi Mai burned herself.

There have been strikes, business licenses returned, resignations of university presidents, deans and professors (40 professors at Hue University), boycotts of classes and refusals to participate in the war. One typically Vietnamese act mentioned earlier has been the carrying of family altars into the streets to oppose tanks, a demonstration of the people's determination to pit the most precious symbols of their traditional values against the instruments of inhumanity and violence.

They Are Determined To Remain Human

Humanist efforts in Vietnam are suppressed by secret police, tear gas, suffocating gas, TNT, grenades, prisons and torture. False nuns and monks inflltrate the Buddhist movement, damaging its prestige and sowing seeds of fear. Extremists are thus encouraged to pervert and destroy the leaders and cadres of non-violent movements. Uncounted numbers of Buddhists and non-Buddhist leaders from all walks of life have been liquidated or sent to prison. In the School of Youth for Social Service, whose only aim is to help the peasants, eight young people have been kidnapped, six killed, eleven seriously wounded. Why? Because they refused to accept American aid or to participate in the war.

The non-violent struggle in Vietnam goes on—amid vast pain and hardship. The world is just beginning to understand that peace everywhere, as well as the future of Vietnam, is linked to this movement. Its success and its contribution to the humanist revolution throughout the world depends upon your understanding and your help.

OTHER WORKS BY THICH NHAT HANH

Vietnam: Lotus in a Sea of Fire (New York: Hill and Wang, 1967).
The Cry of Vietnam (poetry) (Santa Barbara, Calif.: Unicorn Press, 1968).

19 *Abraham J. Heschel*

*Rabbi Abraham J. Heschel, one of the most signifi-
cant religious philosophers and interpreters of Judaism, was a professor at the Jewish Theological
Seminary. In addition to his scholarly work, he
was one of the strongest voices to oppose the war
in Vietnam and was one of the founders of Clergy
and Laity Concerned. He gave the following speech
in March 1938 at a conference of Quaker leaders
in Frankfurt-am-Main, Germany.**

The Meaning
of This Hour

E mblazoned over the gates of the world in
which we live is the escutcheon of the de-
mons. The mark of Cain in the face of man has come to over-
shadow the likeness of God. There has never been so much guilt
and distress, agony, and terror. At no time has the earth been so
soaked with blood. Fellow men turned out to be evil ghosts,
monstrous and weird. Ashamed and dismayed, we ask: Who is
responsible?

History is a pyramid of efforts and errors; yet at times it is the
Holy Mountain on which God holds judgment over the nations.
Few are privileged to discern God's judgment in history. But all
may be guided by the words of the Baal Shem: If a man has
beheld evil, he may know that it was shown to him in order that he
learn his own guilt and repent; for what is shown to him is also
within him.

We have trifled with the name of God. We have taken the ideals
in vain. We have called for the Lord. He came. And was
ignored. We have preached but eluded Him. We have praised but
defied Him. Now we reap the fruits of our failure. Through cen-

turies His voice cried in the wilderness. How skillfully it was trapped and imprisoned in the temples! How often it was drowned or distorted! Now we behold how it gradually withdraws, abandoning one people after another, departing from their souls, despising their wisdom. The taste for the good has all but gone from the earth. Men heap spite upon cruelty, malice upon atrocity.

The horrors of our time fill our souls with reproach and everlasting shame. We have profaned the word of God, and we have given the wealth of our land, the ingenuity of our minds and the dear lives of our youth to tragedy and perdition. There has never been more reason for man to be ashamed than now. Silence hovers mercilessly over many dreadful lands. The day of the Lord is a day without the Lord. Where is God? Why didst Thou not halt the trains loaded with Jews being led to slaughter? It is so hard to rear a child, to nourish and to educate. Why dost Thou make it so easy to kill? Like Moses, we hide our face; for we are afraid to look upon *Elohim,* upon His power of judgment. Indeed, where were we when men learned to hate in the days of starvation? When raving madmen were sowing wrath in the hearts of the unemployed?

Let modern dictatorship not serve as an alibi for our conscience. We have failed to fight *for* right, *for* justice, *for* goodness; as a result we must fight *against* wrong, *against* injustice, *against* evil. We have failed to offer sacrifices on the altar of peace; thus we offered sacrifices on the altar of war. A tale is told of a band of inexperienced mountain climbers. Without guides, they struck recklessly into the wilderness. Suddenly a rocky ledge gave way beneath their feet and they tumbled headlong into a dismal pit. In the darkness of the pit they recovered from their shock only to find themselves set upon by a swarm of angry snakes. For each snake the desperate men slew, ten more seemed to lash out in its place. Strangely enough, one man seemed to stand aside from the fight. When indignant voices of his struggling companions reproached him for not fighting, he called back: "If we remain here, we shall be dead before the snakes. I am searching for a way of escape from the pit for all of us."

Our world seems not unlike a pit of snakes. We did not sink into the pit in 1939, or even in 1933. We had descended into it generations ago, and the snakes have sent their venom into the bloodstream of humanity, gradually paralyzing us, numbing nerve after nerve, dulling our minds, darkening our vision. Good and evil, that were once as real as day and night, have become a blurred mist. In our everyday life we worshiped force, despised compassion, and obeyed no law but our unappeasable appetite. The vision of the sacred has all but died in the soul of man. And when greed, envy and the reckless will to power came to maturity, the serpents cherished in the bosom of our civilization broke out of their dens to fall upon the helpless nations.

The outbreak of war was no surprise. It came as a long-expected sequel to a spiritual disaster. Instilled with the gospel that truth is mere advantage and reverence weakness, people succumbed to the bigger advantage of a lie—"the Jew is our misfortune"—and to the power of arrogance—"tomorrow the whole world shall be ours," "the peoples' democracies must depend upon force." The roar of bombers over Rotterdam, Warsaw, London, was but the echo of thoughts bred for years by individual brains, and later applauded by entire nations. It was through our failure that people started to suspect that science is a device for exploitation, parliaments pulpits for hypocrisy, and religion a pretext for a bad conscience. In the tantalized souls of those who had faith in ideals, suspicion became a dogma and contempt the only solace. Mistaking the abortions of their conscience for intellectual heroism, many thinkers employ clever pens to scold and to scorn the reverence for life, the awe for truth, the loyalty to justice. Man, about to hang himself, discovers it is easier to hang others.

The conscience of the world was destroyed by those who were wont to blame others rather than themselves. Let us remember. We revered the instincts but distrusted the prophets. We labored to perfect engines and let our inner life go to wreck. We ridiculed superstition until we lost our ability to believe. We have helped to extinguish the light our fathers had kindled. We have bartered holiness for convenience, loyalty for success, love for power, wisdom for information, tradition for fashion.

We cannot dwell at ease under the sun of our civilization as our ancestors thought we could. What was in the minds of our martyred brothers in their last hours? They died with disdain and scorn for a civilization in which the killing of civilians could become a carnival of fun, for a civilization which gave us mastery over the forces of nature but lost control over the forces of our self.

Tanks and planes cannot redeem humanity, nor the discovery of guilt by association nor suspicion. A man with a gun is like a beast without a gun. The killing of snakes will save us for the moment but not forever. The war has outlasted the victory of arms as we failed to conquer the infamy of the soul: the indifference to crime, when committed against others. For evil is indivisible. It is the same in thought and in speech, in private and in social life. The greatest task of our time is to take the souls of men out of the pit. The world has experienced that God is involved. Let us forever remember that the sense for the sacred is as vital to us as the light of the sun. There can be no nature without spirit, no world without the Torah, no brotherhood without a father, no humanity without attachment to God.

God will return to us when we shall be willing to let Him in— into our banks and factories, into our Congress and clubs, into our courts and investigating committees, into our homes and theaters. For God is everywhere or nowhere, the Father of all men or no man, concerned about everything or nothing. Only in His presence shall we learn that the glory of man is not in his will to power, but in his power of compassion. Man reflects either the image of His presence or that of a beast.

Soldiers in the horror of battle offer solemn testimony that life is not a hunt for pleasure, but an engagement for service; that there are things more valuable than life; that the world is not a vacuum. Either we make it an altar for God or it is invaded by demons. There can be no neutrality. Either we are ministers of the sacred or slaves of evil. Let the blasphemy of our time not become an eternal scandal. Let future generations not loathe us for having failed to preserve what prophets and saints, martyrs and scholars have created in thousands of years. The apostles of force have shown that they are great in evil. Let us reveal that we can be as great in goodness. We will survive if we shall be as fine and sacrificial in our homes and offices, in our Congress and clubs, as our soldiers are on the fields of battle.

There is a divine dream which the prophets and rabbis have cherished and which fills our prayers, and permeates the acts of true piety. It is the dream of a world, rid of evil by the grace of God as well as by the efforts of man, by his dedication to the task of establishing the kingship of God in the world. God is waiting for us to redeem the world. We should not spend our life hunting for trivial satisfactions while God is waiting constantly and keenly for our effort and devotion.

The Almighty has not created the universe that we may have opportunities to satisfy our greed, envy and ambition. We have not survived that we may waste our years in vulgar vanities. The martyrdom of millions demands that we consecrate ourselves to the fulfillment of God's dream of salvation. Israel did not accept the Torah of their own free will. When Israel approached Sinai, God lifted up the mountain and held it over their heads, saying: "Either you accept the Torah or be crushed beneath the mountain."

The mountain of history is over our heads again. Shall we renew the covenant with God?

OTHER WORKS BY ABRAHAM J. HESCHEL

The Prophets (New York: Harper and Row, 1962).
The Insecurity of Freedom (New York: Farrar, Straus, and Giroux, 1966).
God in Search of Man (New York: Meridian Books, 1961).
Between God and Man (New York: Harper and Row, 1959).

20 *Hermann Hesse*

A German novelist and poet, Hermann Hesse was awarded the Nobel Prize for Literature in 1946. He left Germany during World War I, to protest the violence that was rampant in that country, and became a citizen of Switzerland. The letter below, written in 1917 to a minister of state, challenges him to end the dilemma of war.

Letter to a Minister of State

Tonight, after a strenuous work day, I asked my wife to play a Beethoven sonata for me. This music recalled me from the tension of my business affairs into the only reality we possess, that which causes us pleasure and torment, in which and for which we are living.

Later, I read a few lines in the Book that contains the Sermon on the Mount and the great age-old basic words: "Thou shalt not kill."

But I found no rest. I could neither go to bed nor continue my reading. I was filled with unrest and fear. While I was thinking and searching for the cause, I suddenly remembered a few sentences from a speech of yours, Mr. Minister, which I read during the last few days.

Your speech was sophisticated, but it was not especially new, important or provocative. Condensed to its most important, it said about the same that all speeches of governing members have said for a long time: That we do not wish for anything more fervently than for peace, a new unity, and fruitful work for the future of the people; that we neither want to enrich ourselves nor do we desire to satisfy a lust for murder; that, however, "the moment for negotiations" has not yet arrived. And so for the time being, we must continue bravely to go to war. Any minister of any warring people could give a similar talk—maybe tomorrow or the day after tomorrow.

This speech did not let me sleep tonight, although I have often read similar speeches with the same sad finale and I have slept well afterward. I am sure now that it was the Beethoven sonata—it, and that Book I later read where the wondrous commandments of Sinai and the enlightening words of Christ are written.

Beethoven's music and the words of the Bible said exactly the same to me. It was water from one Source, the only Source from which good comes to man. And suddenly I felt that your speech, Mr. Minister, and the speeches of your governing colleagues, now and then do not stem from this Source; they lack that which makes words valuable and meaningful. Your words lack love; they lack humanity.

Your speech shows a deep feeling of concern and responsibility for your people, for the army of your people, for the honor of your people. But it does not show a feeling for mankind. It means, in brief, a few ten thousand new human sacrifices.

You may possibly call my memories of Beethoven a sentimentality. The words of Christ and of the Bible you will, at least in public, regard with certain reverence. But if you believe in only one of the ideals for which you are fighting this war—be it freedom of countries or of the seas, be it the political progress or the rights of the small nations—if you believe in only one of these ideals, in one of these non-egotistical thoughts in your soul—then, while reading your speech, you must recognize that it has not served this ideal. It has not served any ideal at all. It is not an expression and result of a belief, of a feeling, of a humane need. But, unfortunately, it is only an expression and the result of a dilemma. An understandable dilemma, to be sure, for nothing might be more difficult than to admit a certain disappointment over the results of the war, and to search for the next road to peace—now, today.

Meanwhile, a dilemma, may it be one of ten governments, is something that cannot endure. Over the dilemmas, the necessities will triumph. Somehow, once, it will become necessary for you and all your hostile colleagues—it will be inevitable—to confess the dilemma and to determine to make an end to it.

For the results of war are disappointing to all war lords—today and for some time. No matter who was the victor—here or there —no matter how many prisoners were taken or lost, how much territory was occupied and how much was lost—the result has not been what was expected of war. No solution, no clarity, no decision has come, and none seems to be forthcoming.

To conceal a great dilemma for the time being, for yourself and your people, to postpone great and important decisions (which always demand sacrifices)—that's why you gave your speech, and that's why the other ruling parties give theirs. It's understandable. It is easier for a revolutionary or for a writer than it is for a responsible statesman to recognize the human in a world situation and to draw conclusions from it. It is easier for one of us because we are not responsible for the tremendous depression which grips a people when it realizes that it has not reached its war aim, and it may possibly have sacrificed hundreds of thousands of people and milliards of "values."

But not only for this is it more difficult to admit embarrassment and to foster the end of the war through decisions. It is more difficult for you because you don't listen enough to music, and because you don't read enough in the Bible or the great poets.

This makes you smile. Maybe you also say that you as a private individual have a very close relationship to Beethoven and to everything beautiful and noble. And perhaps you really do. But I really wish that one of these days you would listen to fine music, and suddenly hear the voices that come from these holy sources! I wish that one of these days in a moment of peace you would read a profile of Christ, a poem by Goethe, a saying by Lao-tse.

The moment in which you would do it could become extremely important for the world. Possibly you would find inner freedom. It could be that your eyes and ears would suddenly be opened. Your eyes and ears, Mr. Minister, have been trained for years to see theoretical goals instead of reality; they are—true, it was necessary! —long since used to not seeing a great many of the things of reality, to overlook them, to deny them to yourself.

You know what I mean? Yes, you know. But the voice of a great poet, the voice of the Bible, the eternally clear voice of humanity that speaks to you from this art, maybe it will make you for a moment really see and hear. Ah, what you would see and hear! Nothing any more of a dearth of work and the prices of coal. Nothing any more of tonnage and of pacts, of loans and all the things which have long since become the realities for you. In their place you would see the world, our old patient world, as it lies strewn with corpses and dying, as it is torn and ruined, burnt and defiled. You would see soldiers who lie between the frontiers for days, and how they cannot chase away with their shattered hands the flies from the wounds from which they perish. You would hear the voices of the wounded, the cries of the insane, the clamor and accusations of mothers and fathers, of brides and sisters, the cry of hunger in the people.

If you would hear all this again—what conveniently you were not permitted to hear for months and years—maybe then, with new thoughts, you would comprehend your war aims, your ideals and theories, and test them, and you would really seek to weigh their actual value against the misery of one single month of war, of one single day of war.

If it were only possible to achieve this! This hour of music, this return to the true reality! I know you would hear the voice of humanity. I know you would lock yourself in and cry. And the next day you would go and do what is your duty to humanity. You would forsake a few millions or milliards of money, you would consider a small loss of prestige, you would blow to the winds the thousands of things (things for which in reality you are still fighting alone), if necessary even your seat of Ministry. For it you would do what humanity is pleading for and hopes for from you in untold anguish and misery—you would be the first among the reigning to condemn this lamentable war. You would be the first among the responsible to express what secretly all are already feeling: that a half year, that a month of war, is costlier than all it can gain in return.

Then, Mr. Minister, we would never forget your name, and your deed would mean more to humanity than the deeds of all who have ever led and won the wars.

OTHER WORKS BY HERMANN HESSE

If The War Goes On: Reflections on War and Politics (New York: Farrar, Strauss, and Giroux, '1971).

Siddartha (New York: New Directions, 1951).

Demian (London: Panther Books, 1969).

The Journey to the East (New York: Farrar, Strauss & Giroux, 1968).

21 *Victor Hugo*

Victor Hugo, the great French poet, dramatist and novelist, was active in many of the international peace conferences that were held in the 1840's. His great novel, Les Miserables, *contains within it many of the concepts that have been essential to a deep understanding of non-violence. The following selection * is a speech he delivered in Paris in 1851.*

Address to the
Congres de la Paix

Gentlemen, is this religious idea, universal peace—the linking of the nations together by a common bond, the Gospel, to become the supreme law, mediation to be substituted for war—is this religious idea a practical idea? Is this holy thought one that can be realized? Many practical minds . . . many politicians grown old . . . in the administration of affairs, answer "No." I answer with you; I answer unhesitatingly; I answer "Yes," and I will make an attempt to prove my case later on.

But I will go farther and not only say that it is a realizable end, but that it is an unavoidable end. Its coming can be delayed or hastened; that is all.

The law of the world is not nor can it be different from the law of God. Now, the law of God is not war; it is peace. . . .

When one asserts these high truths, it is quite natural that the assertion should be met with incredulity; it is quite natural that in this hour of our trouble and anguish, the idea of a universal peace should be surprising and shocking, very much like the ap-

* Reprinted from *The Pacifist Conscience*, Peter Mayer, ed. (New York: Holt, Rinehart and Winston, Inc., 1967).

109

parition of the impossible and the ideal. It is quite natural that one should shout "Utopia"; as for me, a modest and obscure worker in this great work of the nineteenth century, I accept this resistance of other minds without being either astonished or disheartened by it. Is it possible that men's minds should not be turned and their eyes blink in a kind of dizziness, when, in the midst of the darkness which still weighs upon us, the radiant door to the future is suddenly thrust open?

Gentlemen, if someone four centuries ago, at a time when war raged from parish to parish, from town to town, from province to province—if someone had said to Lorraine, to Picardy, to Normandy, to Brittany, to Auvergne, to Provence, to Dauphine, to Burgundy, "A day will come when you will no longer wage war, when you will no longer raise men of arms against each other, when it will no longer be said that Normans have attacked the men of Picardy, and the men of Lorraine have driven back those of Burgundy; that you will still have differences to settle, interests to discuss, certainly disputes to solve, but do you know what you will have in place of men on foot and horseback, in place of guns, falconets, spears, pikes, and swords? You will have a small box made of wood, which you will call a ballot box. And do you know what this box will bring forth? An assembly, an assembly in which you will all feel you live, an assembly which will be like your own soul, a supreme and popular council which will decide, judge, and solve everything in law, which will cause the sword to fall from every hand and justice to rise in every heart. And this event will say to you, 'There ends your right, here begins your duty. Lay down your arms! Live in peace!' On that day you will be conscious of a common thought, common interests, and a common destiny. You will clasp each other's hands and you will acknowledge that you are sons of the same blood and the same race. On that day you will no longer be hostile tribes, but a nation. You will no longer be Burgundy, Normandy, Brittany, Provence, you will be France. On that day your name will no longer be war, but civilization."

Well, you say today—and I am one of those who say it with you—all of us here, we say to France, to England, to Prussia, to Austria, to Spain, to Italy, to Russia, we say to them, "A day will come when your weapons will fall from your hands, a day when war will seem absurd and be as impossible between Paris and London, St. Petersburg and Berlin, Vienna and Turin, as today it would seem impossible between Rouen and Amiens, Boston and Philadelphia. A day will come when you France, you Russia, you Italy, you England, you Germany, all you continental nations, without losing your characteristics, your glorious individuality, will intimately dissolve into a superior unity and you will constitute the European brotherhood just as Normandy, Brittany, Burgundy, Lorraine, Alsace, and all our provinces, have dissolved into France. A day will come when there will be no battlefields, but markets opening to commerce and minds opening to ideas. A day will come when the bullets and bombs are replaced by votes, by universal suffrage, by the venerable arbitration of a great supreme senate which will be to Europe what Parliament is to England, the Diet to Germany, and the Legislative Assembly to France. A day will come when a cannon will be a museum-piece, as instruments of torture are today. And we will be amazed to think that these things once existed! A day will come when we shall see those two immense groups, the United States of America and the United States of Europe, stretching out their hands across the sea, exchanging their products, their arts, their works of genius, clearing up the globe, making deserts fruitful, ameliorating creation under the eyes of the Creator, and joining together to reap the well-being of all. . . .

Henceforth the goal of great politics, of true politics, is this: the recognition of all the nationalities, the restoration of the historical unity of nations and the uniting of the latter to civilization by peace, the relentless enlargement of the civilized group, the setting of an example to the still-savage nations; in short, and this recapitulates all I have said, the assurance that justice will have the last word, spoken in the past by might.

RELATED READING BY VICTOR HUGO

Les Miserables (New York: Modern Library Publications, 1961).

22 *Franz Jägerstätter*

An Austrian peasant, Franz Jägerstätter refused to serve in the Nazi army following Germany's invasion of Austria. His courageous and singular refusal was based in a deeply pietistic Catholicism. His story, and his reflections, are a moving testimony to the moral responsibility of the individual as opposed to the obligations of the state. The excerpt that follows * is from a letter written during his imprisonment.

Is There Anything the Individual Can Still Do?

Today one can hear it said repeatedly that there is nothing anymore that an individual can do. If someone were to speak out, it would mean only imprisonment and death. True, there is not much that can be done anymore to change the course of world events. I believe that should have begun a hundred or even more years ago. But as long as we live in this world, I believe it is never too late to save ourselves and perhaps some other soul for Christ. One really has no cause to be astonished that there are those who can no longer find their way in the great confusion of our day. People we think we can trust, who ought to be leading the way and setting a good example, are running along with the crowd. No one gives enlightenment, whether in word or in writing. Or, to be more exact, it may not be given.

* Reprinted from *In Solitary Witness: The Life and Death of Franz Jägerstätter,* by Gordon Zahn. Copyright 1964 by Gordon C. Zahn. Reprinted by permission of Holt, Rinehart and Winston, Inc.

And the thoughtless race goes on, always closer to eternity. As long as conditions are still half-good, we don't see things quite right, or that we could or should do otherwise.

But, alas, once hardship and misery break over us, then it will come to us as with the light of day whether everything the crowd does is so right and good, and then for many the end will pass over into despair.

I realize, too, that today many words would accomplish little more than make one highly eligible for prison. Yet, in spite of this, it is not good if our spiritual leaders remain silent year after year. By "words" I mean, of course, instruction; but example gives direction. Do we no longer want to see Christians who are able to take a stand in the darkness around us in deliberate clarity, calmness, and confidence—who, in the midst of tension, gloom, selfishness, and hate, stand fast in perfect peace and cheerfulness—who are not like the floating reed which is driven here and there by every breeze—who do not merely watch to see what their friends will do but, instead, ask themselves, "What does our faith teach us about this?" or "Can my conscience bear this so easily that I will never have to repent?"

If road signs were ever stuck so loosely in the earth that every wind could break them off or blow them about, would anyone who did not know the road be able to find his way? And how much worse it is if those to whom one turns for information refuse to give him an answer or, at most, give him the wrong direction just to be rid of him as quickly as possible!

23 *Clarence Jordan*

Clarence Jordan, a farmer and biblical scholar, was a prolific writer and experimenter in community. His understanding of the content of Christianity was demonstrated in his Koinonia Farm in Americus, Georgia, an attempt to live in inter-racial harmony and in accordance with the words of Jesus. Taken from a book which offers a contemporary understanding of the teachings of Jesus, this selection * deals with two scriptural passages: "Ye have heard that it was said, An eye for an eye, and a tooth for a tooth: but I say unto you, Resist not him that is evil: but whosoever smiteth thee on thy right cheek, turn to him the other also" (Matthew 5:38-39), and "Ye have heard that it was said, Thou shalt love thy neighbor, and hate thine enemy: but I say unto you, Love your enemies, and pray for them that persecute you" (Matthew 5:43-44).

Things New and Old

We have seen that Jesus thought of the Mosaic laws as disciplines or steps toward the creation of a new society made up of new people. His proclamation of the kingdom or heaven did not destroy the Law but fulfilled it, just as the fruit of a tree does not destroy the blossom but fulfills it, that is, brings it to its highest culmination. Jesus climaxed this thought by pointing out the stages through which the law of retaliation had passed, and how it finally came to rest in the universal love of the Father's own heart.

There were four of these steps, each clearly defined and each

* Reprinted from *Sermon on the Mount* (Valley Forge, Pa.: Judson Press, 1952).

114

progressing toward God's final purpose. First, there was the way of *unlimited retaliation;* second, that of *limited retaliation;* third, that of *limited love;* and fourth, that of *unlimited love.* Let us seek to discover the meaning of each of these steps on the road from retaliation to reconciliation.

The first method of dealing with one's enemies was that of unlimited retaliation. According to this principle, if somebody knocked out one of your eyes, you were justified in knocking out both of his, if you could get to him. If any enemy knocked out one of your teeth, you could knock out his whole set, if you were able. There was no limit placed on revenge. It was the law of the jungle: every man for himself. Like beasts, men would return a bite for a snarl. This philosophy might be expressed thus, "Kill my dog, I'll kill your cat; kill my cat, I'll kill your cow; kill my cow, I'll kill your mule; kill my mule, I'll kill you." It's the same kind of stuff that some civilized, modern nations use today in fanning a minor incident into a full-scale war. The daddy of this idea is the theory that "might makes right." If one has the power to inflict more injury than he receives, he has the right to do so. The main thing is to make sure ahead of time that you have more strength than your enemy. Of course, all the while he'll be making an effort to have more power than you, but it will be a lively contest, even though there might not be any survivors.

It became evident that the end result of this method would be mutual self-destruction. Therefore, a better way was sought, and the law of limited retaliation arose. This principle declared that if one harmed another, "then thou shalt give life for life, eye for eye, tooth for tooth, hand for hand, foot for foot, burning for burning, wound for wound, stripe for stripe." (See Exodus 21:23-25; also Leviticus 24:20; Deuteronomy 19:21.) According to this law, if one knocks out one of your eyes, you must not knock out *both* of his, just one. Or if it's a tooth, you must not retaliate by knocking out *all* of his teeth, just one. In other words, limit your retaliation to the exact amount of the injury. Get even, but no more. Do unto others as they do unto you. This is the attitude that characterizes some modern business organizations. The books must exactly balance, penny for penny, dollar for dollar. It's also what many people have in mind when they speak of "justice." It is the most frequent basis of capital punishment.

Now limited retaliation is a sight better than unlimited retaliation, especially if you're on the receiving end, but Jesus felt that kingdom citizens should go further yet. He said, "You've also heard the saying, 'Take an eye for an eye; take a tooth for a tooth.' But I'm telling you, *never* respond with evil. Instead, if somebody slaps you on your right cheek, offer him the other one too. And if anybody wants to drag you into court and take away your shirt, let him have your undershirt. If somebody makes you go a mile for him, go two miles. Give to him who asks of you, and don't turn your back on anyone who wants a loan" (Matthew 5:38-42, *Cotton Patch Version*). All this adds up to one thing: Let yourself be imposed upon.

The third stage is that of limited love. This method is prescribed in the Old Testament and is referred to by Jesus when he said, "All of you have heard that it was said, 'Love your neighbor and hate your enemy' " (Leviticus 19:18). Some devout Jews might have agreed with Jesus that if your neighbor, i.e., another Jew, knocked out your eye or tooth he might possibly be forgiven, but if he were an enemy, i.e., a Gentile, then he should be given the works. The idea was that there had to be *some* limit to this love and good-will business, and the proper place to draw the line was with your own race. In this way a man could have two standards of righteousness: one in dealing with his kinsmen and another in dealing with strangers. This is what happens invariably in a bi-racial society when the minority group is fairly large. It is the bulwark of prejudice and is echoed in such cries as "white supremacy" and "Herrenvolk." It is also manifested in nationalism, which is merely another form of prejudice, and is back of such slogans as "America for the Americans," not meaning, naturally, the original Americans, the Indians.

To be sure, love, even though limited to one's own circle, is far superior to retaliation, whether limited or unlimited. But Jesus didn't feel that even this brought the law to its final goal, or fulfillment. It was making progress, but would not be complete until it arrived at unlimited love. "But I'm telling you, love the outsiders and pray for those who try to do you in, so that you might be sons of your spiritual Father. For he lets his sun rise on both sinners and saints, and he sends rain on both good people and bad. Listen here, if you love only those who love you, what is your advantage?

Don't even scalawags do that much? And if you speak to no one but your friends, how are you any different? Do not the non-Christians do as much? Now you, you all must be mature, as your spiritual Father is mature" (Matthew 5:44-48, *Cotton Patch Version*).

Here Jesus is simply saying that, for kingdom citizens, love must be the basis of all relationships and that it must be applied universally, both to one's race and nation and to those of other races and nations. There must be no double-dealing, no two-facedness, no partiality. Hate has the same effect upon the personality whether its object is friend or foe. Spiritual traffic cannot be halted at the artificial borders of caste or nation.

Some people rise up to say that this just isn't practical. It might be all right to turn the other cheek to a little baby enemy that can't hit very hard anyway, but it just won't work with a big, bad, grown-up enemy who might knock the daylights out of you. Force is the only language some people can understand (and the only language some people can speak!), so you might as well be realistic about the matter. Suppose you try to be nice to everybody and give to those who ask of you and lend to those who borrow and let the guy who takes the shirt off your back have your undershirt, too, and then they take advantage of you. With human nature being what it is, can you go in for this until everybody is willing to live that way?

Then there are people who say that this attitude is very practical and will work if given a chance. They believe that even in the most cruel person there's a tender spot which will respond to a continuous bombardment of love and good will.

Citing many examples from history, they can present a strong case for the effectiveness of non-retaliation and active love. Many of them are willing to back up their belief in this idea with their lives, which within itself is a strong argument.

The truth might be that in its initial stages unlimited love is very impractical. Folks who are determined enough to hold on to it usually wind up on a cross, like Jesus. Their goods get plundered and they get slandered. Persecution is their lot. Surely nobody would be inclined to call this practical. Yet in its final stages, unlimited love seems to be the only thing that can possibly make any sense. Crucifixions have a way of being followed by resurrections. The end of love seems to be its beginning. Only he who is foolish enough to lose his life finds it. It's the grain of wheat which falls into the ground and *dies* that lives.

But Jesus didn't tell his followers to love their enemies because love would or would not work. The idea probably never occurred to him to raise the question of whether or not it was practical. He told them that they should do it "that they might be sons of their spiritual Father." It was quite evident from the sunshine and rain that the Father didn't limit his love to those who loved him and obeyed him, and it was to be expected that the Son should partake of the Father's nature. This course of conduct would flow as naturally from them as it would from him. Being what he is, God can't help loving all men, regardless of what they are. Even so with God's sons. Their nature is not determined by the reaction of their enemies, but by their relationship to the Father. So in a way, Christians are at the complete mercy of their enemies, since by virtue of their complete surrender to the divine will they no longer have the freedom to cease being what they are. Bound by this higher loyalty, the argument of practicality is irrelevant to them. They do not for the sake of convenience set aside their nature, any more than a minnow transforms itself into a bird when in danger of being swallowed by a bass.

Of course, one does not *have* to be a son of God. It is purely a voluntary matter, though the choice is the difference between life and death. Yet if one does choose to become a son, then one of the conditions is that you "love the outsiders and pray for those who try to do you in." Hate is a denial of sonship, because the Father, not having it in his own nature, never transmits it to his offspring. Or if one confines his love to his own circle, he identifies himself not with God, who loves universally, but with the racketeers and pagans, who limit their love to those who love them.

So Jesus lays upon kingdom citizens the obligation to be "mature, as your heavenly Father is mature." There has been much misunderstanding of this verse because of the translation "perfect" and because the verse is usually considered apart from its context. The Greek word translated "perfect" means to be perfected, or completed, or finished. It means to have all the parts, to have reached full maturity or the desired end. It is the word Jesus used on the cross when he cried, "It is finished." He didn't mean, "This is perfect," but that this was the completion of that phase of his ministry. It had come to its desired end. Paul also uses the word in 1 Corinthians 13:9-10. "For we know by parts and we prophesy by parts, but when that which is complete comes it supersedes that which is partial." Love, being whole, takes precedence over knowledge and prophecy, which are incomplete. Paul likens it to reaching maturity. Love is the adult stage. Without it, people "talk like a baby, think like a baby, act like a baby." Love is that which makes a man "outgrow childish things" and become mature.

This is almost exactly what Jesus means when he says, "Now you, you all must be mature, as your spiritual Father is mature." To talk about unlimited retaliation is babyish; to speak of limited retaliation is childish; to advocate limited love is adolescent; to practice unlimited love is evidence of maturity. It is the Father's desire that his sons become adults like himself.

To be perfect, then, really means to quit acting like a child and to grow up. Is this an impossible command or an unreasonable request for Jesus to make of his followers?

But like the Jew of old who sought a definition of "neighbor" (Luke 10:29), some Christians have been seeking to justify themselves with the question, "And who is my enemy?" An effort is made to classify enemies as personal or national, vicious or gentle, sane or insane, hopeless or redeemable. Unfortunately (or perhaps fortunately), Jesus never answered the question. If he had, he might have told a story like the parable of the "Good Samaritan," except that we perhaps would have called it the "Mean Priest" or the "Horrible Levite."

Nor did Jesus explain just what he meant by love. And Christians are still wondering about it. They wonder if fighting might sometimes be an expression of love, if perhaps certain conditions must be set up prior to exercising love, if there's a personal responsibility when executing a state's orders.

We just don't know all the answers. Even if we did, we couldn't be sure we had all the questions.

Until we know better, a safe guide for the Christian is to love all people. And a good definition of love is that given by Paul in the thirteenth chapter of First Corinthians:

"Love is long-suffering and kind. Love is not envious, nor does it strut and brag. It does not act up, nor try to get things for itself.

It pitches no tantrums, keeps no books on insults or injuries, sees no fun in wickedness, but rejoices when truth prevails. Love is all-embracing, all-trusting, all-hoping, all-enduring. Love never quits" (1 Corinthians 13:4-7, *Cotton Patch Version*).

Without this love, Paul says, it's like looking at your brother through a trick mirror ("through a glass, darkly"). He appears distorted and misshapen and maybe inhuman. But with this love, you see him face to face as he really is. Your knowledge of him is no longer in part, but full. You'll understand him as the Father and the fellowship understand you.

RELATED READING BY CLARENCE JORDAN

The Cotton Patch Versions of the Gospels (3 vols.) (New York: Association Press, 1968-1970).

24 Martin Luther King, Jr.

*Raised in the Southern Baptist tradition and edu-
cated in liberal theology at Boston University, Martin
Luther King, Jr. was a man who met the moment
of crisis and provided for Americans—both black
and white—a leader and a focus of the civil rights
movement in the 1960's. The actions that he led
were deeply committed to non-violence, a non-violence that was greatly influenced by Gandhi. He was
awarded the Nobel Peace Prize in 1964.** *

Suffering and Faith

Some of my personal sufferings over the last few years have also served to shape my thinking. I always hesitate to mention these experiences for fear of conveying the wrong impression. A person who constantly calls attention to his trials and sufferings is in danger of developing a martyr complex and of making others feel that he is consciously seeking sympathy. It is possible for one to be self-centered in his self-denial and self-righteous in his self-sacrifice. So I am always reluctant to refer to my personal sacrifices. But I feel somewhat justified in mentioning them in this article because of the influence they have had in shaping my thinking.

Due to my involvement in the struggle for the freedom of my people, I have known very few quiet days in the last few years. I have been arrested five times and put in Alabama jails. My home has been bombed twice. A day seldom passes that my family and I are not the recipients of threats of death. I have been the victim

* "Suffering and Faith" was reprinted by permission of Joan Daves. Copyright 1960, by the Estate of Martin Luther King, Jr. The excerpts from Dr. King's speeches, were taken from *Soul Force*, the magazine of the Southern Christian Leadership Conference, January, 1972.

of a near-fatal stabbing. So in a real sense I have been battered by the storms of persecution. I must admit that at times I have felt that I could no longer bear such a heavy burden, and have been tempted to retreat to a more quiet and serene life. But every time such a temptation appeared, something came to strengthen and sustain my determination. I have learned now that the Master's burden is light precisely when we take his yoke upon us.

My personal trials have also taught me the value of unmerited suffering. As my sufferings mounted I soon realized that there were two ways that I could respond to my situation: either to react with bitterness or seek to transform the suffering into a creative force. I decided to follow the latter course. Recognizing the necessity for suffering I have tried to make of it a virtue. If only to save myself from bitterness, I have attempted to see my personal ordeals as an opportunity to transform myself and heal the people involved in the tragic situation which now obtains. I have lived these last few years with the conviction that unearned suffering is redemptive.

There are some who still find the cross a stumbling block, and others consider it foolishness, but I am more convinced than ever before that it is the power of God unto social and individual salvation. So like the Apostle Paul I can now humbly yet proudly say, "I bear in my body the marks of the Lord Jesus." The suffering and agonizing moments through which I have passed over the last few years have also drawn me closer to God. More than ever before I am convinced of the reality of a personal God.

Excerpts from Speeches

Whenever I am asked my opinion of the current state of the civil rights movement, I am forced to pause; it is not easy to describe a crisis so profound that it has caused the most powerful nation in the world to stagger in confusion and bewilderment. Today's problems are so acute because the tragic evasions and defaults of several centuries have accumulated to disaster proportions. The luxury of a leisurely approach to urgent solutions—the ease of gradualism—was forfeited by ignoring the issues for too long. The nation waited until the black man was explosive with fury before stirring itself even to partial concern. Confronted now with the interrelated problems of war, inflation, urban decay, white backlash and a climate of violence, it is now *forced* to address itself to race relations and poverty, and it is tragically unprepared. What might once have been a series of separate problems now merge into a social crisis of almost stupefying complexity.

I am not sad that black Americans are rebelling; this was not only inevitable but eminently desirable. Without this magnificent ferment among Negroes, the old evasions and procrastinations would have continued indefinitely. Black men have slammed the door shut on a past of deadening passivity. Except for the Reconstruction years, they have never in their long history on American soil struggled with such creativity and courage for their freedom. These are our bright years of emergence: though they are painful ones, they cannot be avoided.

The first question that the Levite asked was, "If I stop to help this man, what will happen to me?" But then the Good Samaritan came by, and he reversed the question: "If I do not stop to help this man, what will happen to him?"

That's the question before you tonight. Not, "If I stop to help the sanitation workers, what will happen to all of the hours that I usually spend in my office every day and every week as a pastor?" The question is not, "If I stop to help this man in need, what will happen to me?"

"If I do not stop to help the sanitation workers, what will happen to them?" That's the question.

Let us rise up tonight with a greater readiness. Let us stand with a greater determination. And let us move on in these powerful days, these days of challenge, to make America what it ought to be. We have an opportunity to make America a better nation. And I want to thank God, once more, for allowing me to be here with you. . . .

It really doesn't matter what happens now. I left Atlanta this morning, and as we got started on the plane, there were six of us; the pilot said over the public address system, "We are sorry for the delay, but we have Dr. Martin Luther King on the plane. And to be sure that all the bags were checked, and to be sure that nothing would be wrong with the plane, we had to check out everything carefully. And we've had the place protected and guarded all night."

And then I got into Memphis. And some began to say the threats, or talk about the threats that were out. What would happen to me from some of our sick white brothers?

Well, I don't know what will happen now. We've got some difficult days ahead. But it doesn't matter with me now. Because I've been to the mountaintop. And I don't mind. Like anybody, I would like to live a long life. Longevity has its place.

But I'm not concerned about that now. I just want to do God's will. And He's allowed me to go up to the mountain. And I've looked over. And I've seen the promised land. I may not get there with you. But I want you to know tonight, that we, as a people, will get to the promised land. And I'm happy tonight. I'm not worried about anything. I'm not fearing any man. Mine eyes have seen the glory of the coming of the Lord.

There is, deep down within all of us, an instinct—a *Drum Major* instinct, a desire to be out front, a desire to lead the parade, a desire to be first. . . . We all have the *Drum Major* instinct. We all want to be important, to surpass others, to achieve distinction, to lead the parade. . . .

If any of you are around when I have to meet my day, I don't want a long funeral. And if you get somebody to deliver the eulogy, tell him not to talk too long. Every now and then, I wonder what I want them to say.

Tell them not to mention that I have a Nobel Peace Prize. That isn't important. Tell them not to mention that I have three or four hundred other awards. That's not important. Tell them not to mention where I went to school.

I'd like somebody to mention that day, that "Martin Luther King, Jr., tried to give his life serving others." I'd like for somebody

to say that day, that "Martin Luther King, Jr., tried to love somebody." I want you to be able to say that day, that I tried to be right
on the war question. I want you to be able to say that day, that I
did try to feed the hungry. And I want you to be able to say
that day, that I did try in my life to clothe those who were naked.
I want you to say that day, that I did try, in my life, to visit those
who were in prison. I want you to say that I tried to love and serve
humanity.

Yes, if you want to say that I was a *Drum Major,* say that I was
a *Drum Major* for justice, say that I was a *Drum Major* for peace,
that I was a *Drum Major* for righteousness.

Cowardice asks the question, "Is it safe?" Expediency asks the
question, "Is it politic?" Vanity asks the question, "Is it popular?"
But conscience asks the question, "Is it right?" And there comes a
time when one must take a position that is neither safe, nor politic,
nor popular, but he must take it because his conscience tells him
that it is right. . . .

I can't segregate my moral concern. We are engaged in a war
where we are the aggressors. And I think it's necessary to say to
the policy-makers of our country that we are wrong. We should
admit to the world that we made a tragic mistake in Vietnam.

OTHER WORKS BY MARTIN LUTHER KING, JR.

The Trumpet of Conscience (New York: Harper and Row, 1968).
Strength To Love (New York: Harper and Row, 1963).
Why We Can't Wait (New York: Harper and Row, 1964).
Where Do We Go From Here: Chaos or Community? (New York:
Harper and Row, 1967).

25 Thomas Merton

*A Trappist monk, Thomas Merton was one of the strongest voices in the 1960's writing on a theology of non-violence and speaking against the evils of our society. Merton strongly influenced many of the contemporary Catholics active in peace and social justice today. He himself was influenced by Aldous Huxley, Erasmus and Gandhi. The following excerpt * is from an article that Merton wrote for the 1968 PAX Conference, shortly before his death later that year.*

Peace and Revolution

One of the main themes of *Ulysses* is the breakdown of language and of communication as part of the disruption of Western culture. The extraordinary linguistic richness of the book—which however comes out mostly in parody—only reminds us more forcefully how much further the breakdown has gone in the last fifty years. Pacifism and non-violence are fully and consciously involved in this question of language. Non-violence, as Gandhi conceived it, is in fact a kind of language. The real dynamic of non-violence can be considered as a purification of language, a restoration of true communication on a human level, when language has been emptied of meaning by misuse and corruption. Non-violence is meant to communicate love not in word but in act. Above all, non-violence is meant to convey and to defend truth which has been obscured and defiled by political double-talk.

The real lesson for us is this: we must clearly understand the function of non-violence against the background of the collapse of

* Reprinted from *Peace* Magazine, Volume III, Fall/Winter, 1968/1969.

language. It is no accident that Noam Chomsky, a leader in the draft resistance movement, is also an expert in the study of language. The special force of the Cyclops episode in *Ulysses* is that it shows how the language of pacifism and the language of force can both fit with equal readiness into a context of linguistic corruption. We have to be terribly aware of the fact that our pacifism and non-violence can easily be nothing more than parodies of themselves. We must recognize the temptation to be quite content with this—to be content to express our weak convictions in weak and provisional terms, meanwhile waiting for an opportunity to abandon non-violence altogether and go over to the side of force, on the ground that we have tried non-violence and found it wanting.

Has non-violence been found wanting? Yes and no. It has been found wanting wherever it has been the non-violence of the weak. It has not been found so when it has been the non-violence of the strong. What is the difference? It is a difference of language. The language of spurious non-violence is merely another, more equivocal form of the language of power. It is a different method of expressing one's will to power. It is used and conceived pragmatically, in reference to the seizure of power. But that is not what non-violence is about. Non-violence is not for power but for truth. It is not pragmatic but prophetic. It is not aimed at immediate political results, but at the manifestation of fundamental and crucially important truth. Non-violence is not primarily the language of efficacy, but the language of *kairos*. It does not say "We shall overcome" so much as "This is the day of the Lord, and whatever may happen to us, *He* shall overcome."

And this, of course, is the dimension that is entirely absent from the Cyclops episode in *Ulysses*. Unhappily, it is too often absent from our world and our practice today. As a result people begin to imagine that to say "only force works" is to discredit non-violence. This half-truth—that only force is efficacious—may turn out to be one of the most dangerous illusions of our time. It may do more than anything else to promote an irresponsible and meaningless use of force in a pseudo-revolution that will only consolidate the power of the police state. Never was it more necessary to understand the importance of genuine non-violence as a power for real change because it is aimed not so much at revolution as at conversion. Unfortunately, mere words about peace, love and civilization have completely lost all power to change anything.

OTHER WORKS BY THOMAS MERTON

Faith and Violence (Notre Dame, Ind.: University of Notre Dame Press, 1968).

Gandhi on Non-Violence (New York: New Directions Publishing Co., 1965).

Seeds of Destruction (New York: Farrar, Straus & Giroux, 1965).

Contemplation in a World of Action (Garden City, N.Y.: Doubleday, 1971).

Thomas Merton on Peace (New York: McCall Publishing Co., 1971).

Redeeming the Time (London: Burns and Oates, 1966).

26 *Perry Muckerheidi*

Perry Muckerheidi has spent the last few years in Milwaukee coordinating youth's commitment to hunger and directing the Walk from Hunger Campaigns. He wrote and produced Miles to Go, *an enthusiastic and spirited documentary of the walks. In mid-summer 1971 he began filing his C.O. Statement and shared his thoughts and reflections with the editor of this volume. The Prologue is included below.*

I Believe

I believe in God.
I believe in Jesus Christ.
I believe in Man.

I believe in God as the infinite power which is the reason for my
    being.
I believe in Jesus Christ as major revelation of God.
I believe in man as the house of God, created in his image.

I believe that my finite person is incapable of ever comprehending
    the infinite, yet God reveals himself to me daily through
    myself and relations with others, through the lives of men
    and women throughout history, and ultimately through
    the life of Christ.
I believe that through Jesus Christ, the man from Nazareth, God
    reveals to me the life I should live.
I believe God lives within me and all of mankind.

I believe the basis of life is love: love of oneself, love of one's neigh-
    bor, and as Christ has said, love of one's enemies.

I believe we are meant to live in harmony.

I believe that when we seek this harmony with the motivations of love, we glorify God as he has commanded.

I believe in the basic law of God: Thou shall not kill.

I believe in the basic law of God: Thou shall have no other gods before me.

I believe that since God lives within each of us and all of us, the service of man is the service of God; therefore the destruction of man is the profaning of God.

I believe in non-violence as witnessed by the life of Christ.

I believe the laws of man must become secondary when they conflict with the natural laws of God.

I believe life must be a witness.

I believe this witness must be total, a commitment of all one's talents to the glory of God.

I believe this witness must work to overcome national, racial, economic, political and cultural divisions to unite mankind in peace.

I believe the way of God is the way witnessed by Christ which is the way of peace.

I believe peace is found through its pursuit.

I believe God is revealed through the pursuit of peace.

I believe to search for the revelations of God is to work to know God.

I believe to seek God is to know God.

I believe God reveals himself through the revelations of the soul.

I believe the soul is revealed through the process of the search for it.

I believe the search takes many individual and collective forms.

I believe it is found in the development of creativity which is within all of us, which we must work to free for the collective use in the service of man, which is again the revelation of God.

I believe it is most found in the service of my fellow man as witnessed by the life of Christ, the man closest to God.

I believe just as Christ's life is a witness to the laws of God, my life

must be a witness to my search of him through my service
to man.

I believe therefore that I could not kill another man nor could I in
good conscience serve or involve myself in any system,
nor support in any way, the creation or continuation of
any process which seeks to or results in the killing of another man.

27 *A. J. Muste*

During his lifetime, A. J. Muste was regarded as one of the most prominent spokesmen for the pacifist movement in America. He wavered in the mid-1930's, believing violence to be an effective means for change, but after 1936 he was reconverted to the validity of a religious-based pacifism, as the following selection * indicates.

The Workability of Non-Violence

There are two ultimate questions we must now consider. If we may use a military figure to state a pacifist case, we can say that one is the question of what we fight *for;* the other of what we fight *with* and rely on for a sense of security.

Paradoxically, life is worth living for those who have something for which they will gladly give up life. Individuals and nations need something beyond themselves to which they give unconditional homage and devotion. A nation cannot exist if it has no purpose save to exist, to survive at any cost and on any terms. It needs a spiritual goal. In the words of the Psalmist, "Except the Lord build the city, they labor in vain that build it."

It is equally true that in the final analysis the weapons with which a nation must fight are spiritual. Its defense and security are spiritually based, or they do not really exist. Even military men recognize that without morale, a spiritual factor, the biggest and best equipped army in the world is a shell. In answer to the question, "What constitutes the bulwark of our own liberty and

* Reprinted by permission of Fellowship Publications.

132

independence?" Lincoln replied: "It is not our frowning battle-
ments, our bristling sea coasts, our army and our navy. These are
not our reliance against tyranny. *All of these may be turned against
us without making us weaker for the struggle. . . . Our defense is
in the spirit which prized liberty as the heritage of all men, in all
lands, everywhere."*

A people thus devoted to a spiritual goal and thus skilled in
wielding spiritual weapons would have immense driving and stay-
ing power. It would have a faith that other peoples, especially the
long down-trodden masses, could embrace in place of the Communist faith that has so vast an attraction for them now. . . .

The Western world in its concept of democracy, the United
States in "the American dream," and Christians in their gospel
and ethic of love, of evil, overcome not by evil but by good, have
knowledge of such a spiritual goal. The difficulty is that we do not
pursue this goal. On the one hand are a lot of ordinary folks who
have never truly been taught that there are other, better means for
dealing with Communism than the shooting-mad-dogs technique.
There are the hard-boiled who have no scruples. Then there are the
many varieties of sophisticated intellectual and spiritual leaders.
These people, however they phrase it in words, think that it is
pointless, at least in this modern age, to call upon governments and
nations to behave ethically, not to mention in a Christian way, to
repent of the sins of atomic and biological war and to trust in
God. With the chanting of the magic word "utopianism," these
people dismiss the challenge and the hope of building brotherhood
on earth as in heaven. Alas, not a few peace-workers are among
them, placing their reliance on some device by which an unrepentant and essentially unbelieving nation will on the basis of self-
interest work out an agreement with an unrepentant and avowedly
unbelieving Communist regime that will bring peace!

On the other hand, if in any typical Protestant church of a Sunday morning I were to say pretty much what I have here been
writing about centering our national policy around the needy children of the world, Christian hearts would be touched and Christian heads would be nodded gravely in assent. And then, as the
Roper polls show, these good Christian folk would agree nearly
to the man that it is also right and wise for the United States to keep
adding to the H-bomb stockpile as the best way to keep the godless,

Christ-denying Communists from coming over here and closing Christ's churches!

Two pastors of the French Reformed Church were put into a concentration camp during World War II for refusal to conform to anti-Semitic laws enacted by the Pétain regime. The Communists in the camp were impressed by the two men who seemed to them to behave like early Christians, for they accepted a second imprisonment in the camp rather than sign a piece of paper promising obedience to collaborationist laws, though few got a second chance to get out of a concentration camp in those days. "Why should anybody hesitate to sign a piece of paper, even if it tells a lie?" was the Communist reaction.

So impressed were they, in fact, that they began to spend several hours every day with the pastors in studying the New Testament. When the pastors were on the point of being released again, one of the Communists said to them in parting: "We recognize that your faith is superior to ours. This way of life which Jesus taught and lived everybody ought to live. And everybody will," he added, "after the revolution."

The problem of morale and faith facing the West is here vividly laid bare. It is that the Christian nations, Christian churches, Christian people are in thorough agreement with that Communist. Again the "enemy" is ourselves. We and that Communist are agreed that the Christian faith and way are superior; agreed that someday it has to prevail; and agreed that this will come to pass after we—Communists and Christians—have made it possible for our ways of life to survive and prevail by our respective impure and violent means. The Communists believe it will come to pass "after the revolution" when they are in control. American Christians believe it will come after they by the threat or use of their atomic arsenal have got things under control. But they all unite in the grand chorus: "But it isn't practical *now!*"

At an earlier stage we found that it is not possible to be absorbed at one and the same time in the power struggle and in the task of spreading general well-being across the world and building a stable world economy. We are faced with a choice of goals.

A choice of means must likewise be made, however we may shrink from it. Our firm conviction as pacifists is that it is not possible to achieve democracy by undemocratic means, to overcome Communism by resorting increasingly to Communist methods, to save the values of Christian civilization by throwing them overboard as modern war requires us to do. On the positive side it is our conviction that love translated into concrete action for human brotherhood is the way to overcome evil and that the spiritual power which flows through men when they give themselves to God in faith and obedience is real and the most potent force in the universe.

In this context we always come up against the question, "Will it work?" Will it work with the Russians, the Communists, the totalitarians? In the abstract and in general people are usually willing to grant the pacifist case, but the concrete enemy of the moment is always a *special* case. Nor would pacifists deny that totalitarianism in its modern forms and equipped with modern weapons of thought control, regimentation and terrorism presents a tremendous challenge to pacifists. It does also to the advocates of any other method for meeting aggression and tyranny, a point which non-pacifists sometimes overlook. Their record, as we pointed out at length in the beginning of this essay, is not one of success!

But what is the pacifist's answer to the question of workability? We are now dealing with the problem of practicality on another level than a short way back when we were dealing with the political-economic approach versus the military. There it was a question of "calculated risk," and we argued that on that basis the chances were that if the United States continued in the power struggle and armaments race, it would lose the battle against Communism. If, on the contrary, it embarked on a policy of devoting its skills and resources to developing a sound global economy, it would probably win. Now we are dealing with moral or spiritual values. In Christian terms we are proposing that men apply Christ's method of uncalculating love, of feeding the enemy and so on, rather than depending upon the sword for defense or liberation.

Stating the matter in other terms, we are here thinking of the morally responsible human being. All who believe in some kind of moral order, whether or not they are Christians or consider themselves religious at all, face a crucial problem in connection with war. The question is not whether one is going to die in war; at the appointed time all men, and nations also, die. This is in the order of nature. The question for the morally responsible being is what happens to *himself* if he becomes a murderer, drops atomic bombs on little enemy children instead of trying to bring them food and healing. The question is what *moral* price he is prepared to pay for his country's victory in war.

When on this level the Christian is asked whether the way of uncalculating love—of not "offending one of these little ones" behind the Iron Curtain—"works" in some immediate political sense, his first answer is bound to be that he doesn't think this is any of his business. God whom he knows in Christ commands love. He does not promise success to today's Christian any more than he did to Jesus. Indeed, there is sure to be a cross in the picture somewhere. One of the signs that we are off the track is that everything goes smoothly and all men speak well of us. When the Christian asks God for victory, success, a blank check, he has ceased to believe in God.

The morally responsible person will give essentially the same answer. He has to be true, in the final pinch, to the highest that he knows. He has to be able to live with himself. If his moral standard amounts to obeying whatever orders some government gives him (remember the Nuremberg doctrine of the guilt of *individual* Nazis) or if his standard is what he can get away with, then he is no longer a moral being. This is why, in fact, any human being not bereft of sanity altogether "draws a line somewhere," at some point says, "I can do no other."

The modern pacifist draws the line at participation in atomic and bacteriological war. When he is asked whether this pacifism is "politically effective," his reply is: "If human beings do not draw this line, then where will they draw the line? What are they waiting for?" In the great drama, *Jakobowski and the Colonel*, Jakobowski, the refugee, says to the Nazi colonel who has just been engaged in torturing certain victims: "There is one advantage that the hunted has over the hunter—namely, that he is not the hunter." The advantage is an ultimate one: not to join the hunters. If a man loses it, there is nothing to compensate for the loss.

Totalitarian regimes do indeed present a grave problem, and our argument in no sense proceeds on the basis of minimizing the evil of such regimes. But the familiar argument that Gandhi could get by with non-violence in dealing with the British but that non-violence is no good in dealing with this or that other regime in practice means that *any* methods have to be used with the latter. This clearly means surrender of the moral life. It is capitulation to the amoral or antimoral philosophy of Bolshevism: any means is justified because *my* end is good. Indeed, it is to fall lower than this in the moral scale because it amounts to saying: "The mere survival of my country at any cost and by any means in a naked struggle for power is justified." It is to enthrone the doctrine of military necessity as the moral imperative and to deny, utterly and finally, that "he who seeketh his life shall lose it."

There is a curious quirk in the thinking of people today. They will witness several world wars, as my generation has, and yet continue preparations for atomic and biological war, having from experience of the loss of life involved in past wars a frightening notion of what human as well as material cost future war will entail. Then somebody proposes that non-violence would be a better way and they say, "But somebody might get killed!"

This familiar argument shows what an almost unbreakable hold the war pattern has on the thinking of people. Somehow the slaughter of untold millions in war seems rational or inevitable to them and "somebody might get killed" is conclusive ground for giving no further thought to a method the efficacy of which Gandhi demonstrated in at least one great political struggle. In almost any other realm, people would have open minds to some further experimenting with the new method. In this realm the U.S. government will have a $50,000,000 military budget and not appropriate a nickel for research in non-violence, and many persons, including intellectual and spiritual leaders, either accept this outright or then go along after making a feeble protest which is dignified as "critical support of the war policy." What a rut for thinking to be in at what is probably the most critical moment in human history. What *faith* in material things and military means is here revealed!

If men are not willing to practice the way of non-violence with the same kind of commitment and recklessness of cost or consequences as they practice the way of war and as Communists work for Communism, clearly non-violence will not work.

OTHER WORKS BY A. J. MUSTE

The Essays of A. J. Muste, Nat Hentoff, ed. (Indianapolis, Ind.: Bobbs-Merrill Co., 1967).
Not by Might (New York: Harper and Row, 1947).

Non-Violence in an Aggressive World (New York: Harper and Bros., 1940).

Peace Agitator: The Story of A. J. Muste (New York: Macmillan Co., 1963).

28 *William Penn*

William Penn became a member of the Quakers in England, and was jailed because of his radical stance. Despite this, he was given proprietorship over the colony of Pennsylvania. Under his direction, and because of his strong stand of non-violence, relations between the settlers and the Indians remained peaceful and harmonious, the only situation in the new land where this harmony prevailed. The following selection,* written in 1681, well illustrates this.

First Letter to the Delaware Indians

My Friends—There is one great God and power that hath made the world and all things therein, to whom you and I, and all people owe their being and well-being, and to whom you and I must one day give an account for all that we do in the world; this great God hath written his law in our hearts, by which we are taught and commanded to love and help, and do good to one another, and not to do harm and mischief one to another. Now this great God hath been pleased to make me concerned in your parts of the world, and the king of the country where I live hath given unto me a great province, but I desire to enjoy it with your love and consent, that we may always live together as neighbors and friends; else what would the great God say to us, who hath made us not to devour and destroy one another, but live soberly and kindly together in the world? Now I would have you well observe, that I am very sensible of the unkind-

* Reprinted from *Nonviolence in America: A Documentary History*, Staughton Lynd, ed. (Indianapolis, Ind.: The Bobbs-Merrill Company, Inc., 1966).

ness and injustice that hath been too much exercised toward you by the people of these parts of the world, who sought themselves, and to make great advantages by you, rather than be examples of justice and goodness unto you, which I hear hath been a matter of trouble to you, and caused great grudgings and animosities, sometimes to the shedding of blood, which hath made the great God angry. But I am not such a man, as is well known in my own country; I have great love and regard toward you, and I desire to win and gain your love and friendship, by a kind, just and peaceable life, and the people I send are of the same mind, and shall in all things behave themselves accordingly; and if in anything any shall offend you or your people, you shall have a full and speedy satisfaction for the same, by an equal number of just men on both sides, that by no means you may have just occasion of being offended against them. I shall shortly come to you myself, at what time we may more largely and freely confer and discourse of these matters. In the meantime, I have sent my commissioners to treat with you about land, and a firm league of peace. Let me desire you to be kind to them and the people, and receive these presents and tokens which I have sent to you, as a testimony of my good will to you, and my resolution to live justly, peaceably, and friendly with you.

I am your loving friend,

William Penn

RELATED READING

No Cross, No Crown (Wallingford, Pa.: Pendle Hill Publications, 1944).
An Essay Towards the Present and Future Peace of Europe (New York: Carnegie Endowment for International Peace, 1943).

29 Popes, Bishops, Councils

The late Pope John XXIII, one of the greatest spiritual and social influences in the century, left a great legacy in his encyclical Pacem in Terris, *an excerpt of which is printed below, and in the spirit of Vatican Council II which he convened and which was continued by his successor Pope Paul VI, a portion of whose encyclical* The Development of Peoples *is also given. Included here too are excerpts from Vatican Council II's* Constitution on the Church in the Modern World, *the National Council of Catholic Bishops'* Justice in the World, *and a statement of American bishops made in the fall of 1971.*

Pacem in Terris

Since the right to command is required by the moral order and has its source in God, it follows that, if civil authorities legislate for or allow anything that is contrary to the will of God, neither the law made nor the authorization granted can be binding on the consciences of the citizens since God has more right to be obeyed than men.

Ban Nuclear Weapons

Therefore, in this age which boasts of its atomic power, it is irrational to believe that war is still an apt means of vindicating violated rights. . . . Justice then, right reason, and humanity urgently demand that the arms race should be reduced equally and simultaneously by the parties concerned. Nuclear weapons should be banned.

Co-Existence of Political Systems

It must be borne in mind, furthermore, that neither can false philosophical teachings regarding the nature, origin and destiny of the universe and of man be identified with historical movements that have economic, social, cultural or political ends, not even when these movements have originated from these teachings and have drawn and still draw inspiration therefrom. Because the teachings, once they are drawn up and defined, remain always the same, while the movements, working on historical situations in constant evolution, cannot but be influenced by these latter and cannot avoid, therefore, being subject to changes, even of a profound nature. Besides, who can deny that these movements, insofar as they conform to the dictates of right reason and are interpreters of the lawful aspirations of the human person, contain elements that are positive and deserving of approval.

Constitution on the Church in the Modern World

Motivated by the same spirit, we cannot fail to praise those who renounce the use of violence in the vindication of their rights and who resort to methods of defense which are otherwise available to weaker parties too, provided this can be done without injury to the rights and duties of others or of the community itself.

Obedience No Excuse

Contemplating this melancholy state of humanity, the Council wishes, above all things else, to recall the permanent binding force of universal natural law and its all-embracing principles. Man's conscience itself gives ever more emphatic voice to these principles. Therefore, actions which deliberately conflict with these same principles, as well as orders commanding such actions, are criminal, and blind obedience cannot excuse those who yield to them.

Conscientious Objection

Moreover, it seems right that laws make humane provision for the case of those who for reasons of conscience refuse to bear arms, provided, however, that they agree to serve the human community in some other way.

Ban on Indiscriminate Destruction

The men of our time must realize that they will have to give a somber reckoning of their deeds of war, for the course of the future will depend greatly on the decisions they make today. With these truths in mind, this most Holy Synod makes its own the condemnation of total war already pronounced by recent popes, and issues the following declaration: "Any act of war aimed indiscriminately at the destruction of entire cities or extensive areas along with their population is a crime against God and man himself. It merits unequivocal and unhesitating condemnation."

The Development of Peoples

"God intended the earth and all that it contains for the use of every human being and people. Thus, as all men follow justice and unite in charity, created goods should abound for them on a reasonable basis." All other rights whatsoever, including those of property and of free commerce, are to be subordinated to this principle.

Property

To quote Saint Ambrose: "You are not making a gift of your possessions to the poor person. You are handing over to him what is his. For what has been given in common for the use of all, you have arrogated to yourself. The world has given to all, and not only to the rich." That is, private property does not constitute for anyone an absolute and unconditioned right. No one is justified in keeping for his exclusive use what he does not need, when others lack necessities. In a word, "according to the traditional doctrine as found in the Fathers of the Church and the great theologians, the right to property must never be exercised to the detriment of the common good." If there should arise a conflict "between acquired private rights and primary community exigencies," it is the responsibility of public authorities "to look for a solution, with the active participation of individuals and social groups."

Temptation to Violence

There are certainly situations whose injustice cries to heaven. When whole populations destitute of necessities live in a state of dependence barring them from all initiative and responsibility, and all opportunity to advance culturally and share in social and political life, recourse to violence, as a means to right these wrongs to human dignity, is a grave temptation.

Justice in the World

Let recognition be given to the fact that international order is rooted in the inalienable rights and dignity of the human being. Let the United Nations' Declaration of Human Rights be ratified by all governments who have not yet adhered to it, and let it be fully observed by all.

War/Non-Violence

It is absolutely necessary that international conflicts should not be settled by war, but that other methods better befitting human nature should be found. Let a strategy of non-violence be fostered also, and let conscientious objection be recognized and regulated by law in each nation.

This priority of love in history draws other Christians to prefer the way of non-violent action and work in the area of public opinion.

Ancient divisions between nations and empires, between races and classes, today possess new technological instruments of destruction. The arms race is a threat to man's highest good, which is life; it makes poor peoples and individuals yet more miserable, while making richer those already powerful; it creates a continuous danger of conflagration, and in the case of nuclear arms it threatens to destroy all life from the face of the earth.

Wealth

Our faith demands of us a certain sparingness in use, and the Church is obliged to live and administer its own goods in such a way that the Gospel is proclaimed to the poor. If instead the Church appears to be among the rich and the powerful of this world its credibility is diminished.

We have nevertheless been able to perceive the serious injustices which are building around the world of men a network of domination, oppression and abuses which stifle freedom and which keep the greater part of humanity from sharing in the building up and enjoyment of a more just and more fraternal world.

Unless combatted and overcome by social and political action, the influence of the new industrial and technological order favors the concentration of wealth, power and decision-making in the hands of a small public or private controlling group.

Statement of American Bishops

In the light of the Gospel and from an analysis of the Church's teaching on conscience, it is clear that a Catholic can be a conscientious objector to war in general or to a particular war "because of religious training and belief." It is not enough, however, simply to declare that a Catholic can be a conscientious objector or a selective conscientious objector. Efforts must be made to help Catholics form a correct conscience in the matter, to discuss with them the duties of citizenship, and to provide them with adequate draft counseling and information services in order to give them the full advantage of the law protecting their rights. Catholic organizations which could qualify as alternative service agencies should be encouraged to support and provide meaningful employment for the conscientious objector. As we hold individuals in high esteem who conscientiously serve in the armed forces, so also should we regard conscientious objection and selective conscientious objection as positive indicators within the Church of a sound moral awareness and respect for human life.

Vietnam

At this point in history it seems clear to us that whatever good we hope to achieve through continued involvement in this war is now outweighed by the destruction of human life and of moral values which it inflicts. It is our firm conviction, therefore, that the speedy ending of this war is a moral imperative of the highest priority. Hence, we feel a moral obligation to appeal urgently to our nation's leaders and indeed to the leaders of all nations involved in this tragic conflict to bring the war to an end with no further delay.

Amnesty

Those who in good conscience resisted this war are also subjects of our genuine pastoral concern. They too must be reintegrated as fully as possible into our society and invited to share the opportunities and responsibilities of building a better nation. Hence we repeat our plea of October 21, 1971 that the civil authorities grant generous pardon of convictions incurred under the Selective Service Act, with the understanding that sincere conscientious objectors should remain open in principle to some form of service to the community. Surely a country which showed compassion by offering amnesty after the Civil War will want to exercise no less compassion today.

30 *Rod Skenandore*

One of the very impressive spokesmen for the American Indian Movement, Rod Skenandore was one of the prime resource people at the Young World Development's National Conversation during the summer of 1971. He delivered "An Indian Prayer" during the conference, one of the most moving moments for the gathering.

An Indian Prayer: A Proposal to Man

For a long time now, I have questioned what you taught me in your schools. The words I learned from your books have taken on new meanings and, each year I have lived, new concepts and ideas have shaped in my mind so that now, I constantly look back and remember all those words.

I remember you saying in your stuffy, sweaty classrooms that all men are created equal. And, as a youth, you also had me believe that you felt the same way. As I sat there dreaming of the trees, the deer, the coyote and the wolf, as well as all the other animals that were here before you and I, I nearly accepted the falsehoods you perpetrated and I came close to believing what you said to be true. But, while I dreamt, my mind was closed, for even then somehow, I could not accept your strange beliefs, and now in my state of manhood, I am well aware of the fact that you were not only wrong in selection of yourself as a teacher over me simply because you could not find the necessary level of intelligence needed to understand my culture, but you were wrong as well in telling me I was ignorant because I found it hard to understand your language. A language I did not need, for you see, I already had a language that suited all my needs. And even then, I sat and watched as your own youth struggled to make sense out of that language; yet because of your impatient persistence, you told me I was below comprehension and had no right in my own land.

I sadden at the thought that in all this time, you still cannot see who was really wrong. . . . Of course, it could have been due to the fact that because you thought I was ignorant and incapable, I would not figure it out for myself and you could go onward unexposed. But the truth is I knew all along, almost from that first time so long ago, when the first weary, dirty men came off their rotting boats that sat low in the water, nervously tugging at their vermin infested beards, that you were here simply because you, as exiled men, had no place else to go. And because of this, and because at the time there was plenty here for all, I let you stay.

Maybe you felt if you could teach me equality in the way you reasoned, then because of this and your eloquent way of saying things, I would accept you more readily and that I as an ignorant savage, as you so wrongly visioned me, would be pleased at your attempts and with praise would flock to your door in search of wisdom . . . or maybe you felt that if I accepted the terms you so thoughtfully laid out in your Constitution, I would overlook the fact that you were killing my people in much the same manner only ten-fold the amount, as you did your own kind back in the country you had just fled to avoid prosecution of these crimes against man. Then taking the remainder of my people who had avoided the onslaught you perpetrated, you marched them long distances, at the worst times of the year to the worst parts of the country, and closed them off in concentration camps with the promise of eternal protection from enemies of foreign lands when all the while, the real enemy I had to face was in fact already here.

Over the long stifling years of summer and winter, spring and fall, I watched as you slowly but surely began to methodically take over, never once remembering that as an agreement of men, you have made treaties with me in order to live on my land, treaties you never honored, and watching you and seeing you, as you constantly attempted to out-do the other, I saw your narrow ways were humorous and I learned to laugh.

At these times, however, I wished that for the sake of all mankind as well as for the sake of you as a people alienated, you would stop your show of destruction and would soon realize that it was your greed which had caused this destruction, for surely, if you remained in ignorance of all this wrong, you would soon begin to fear one another and this would result in an overall hate. Now, all I can see is the fact that all people live in fear of living in fear.

As I walked among the spirits of nature, I saddened by the slow unnecessary death that even then, by your presence, the mother earth was having to accept. I watched as the once clean dirt where I left my moccasin prints soiled and grew heavy with the pieces of steel and bits of broken glass you so carelessly left lying in your abandoned paths. As a result of this, I soon found a reason to wear the shoes you made with the thick soles. And the form-fitting gloves you fashioned from the hides of the countless buffalo you so joyously slaughtered soon found a place in my life. For, in your attempt to close off the parcels of land you now fancied as your own, I was forced to protect the scant remainder you had left by applying the same methods of barbed wire as you.

And I could not help but shudder as I saw you throw yourself headlong into a search for power. For it seemed that your concept of power was: whoever has the most weapons will survive, and one day I awoke from a dream. My eyes filled with smoke. My ears hurt from the silence of death, and my heart burst with loss. For as I stood to meet the morning, bodies of my people lay scattered like burned seeds never allowed to grow. And suddenly, the earth felt strange beneath my feet as I walked amongst the dead mixing tears with the blood on the faces of small babies. And, after you fired your first shot, the first in this nation, the echo of its thunderous death has not faded but has rippled across the waters to find new sounding walls, and as a result, I've watched as you prepared your own youth for wars by telling them that if they did not stand up and volunteer to fight and die for their country, then in time, invaders from foreign lands would come and take away all they had. I guess you were afraid that someone else would do the same things to you that you had done to me.

I was here too when you told your people that I was an invader in this land also. And that I had come from an ice-ladened land far to the north, crossing that ice as well, and eventually finding my way here. But, if you were realistic, you would see that the time you said it took for me to make my journey was absurd, for I could never have survived the bitter cold. And also, I was there on that date so long ago when you stood on platforms proclaiming your own conceived right to this land by stating "Fourscore and seven years ago . . ." And I knew then that you had planned to stay as you named a man of your own kind by calling him the father of the country.

In spite of all your beliefs, I have been here all the while. I never arrived as you so commonly refer to, for, you see, I was already here, living in nature the way nature had provided. The deer and the wolf, the elk and the bear, were all my brothers, and when they saw that I was in need, they gave of themselves. And when I went out to seek visions of tomorrow, they gathered around and provided warmth. But when your people began to kill them off without concern and in the name of sportsmanship, they stood at my door and bid farewell, explaining that they could no longer trust even me, for I was a man and they had seen what man would do to one another.

Now, my white-skinned brothers, I am tired. The spirits of my ancestors are tired. And now they tell me that the time for hate and destruction, wars and death is over. They tell me that if I wait too long to tell you of these things, all the time needed to cause change will slip away and I too will face the same destiny you seem to be seeking. They tell me to take the words you taught me in your schools and to somehow make you understand what you are doing and seem to persist in doing. They tell me that if I am to live on in the way of my ancestors in harmony to life, I must take back my way of living and protecting my own people. I must reconstruct my old ways and must have control over my own destiny. They tell me, also, that I must live as a separate nation in my own country, and that you, as brothers as well as the creators and controllers of money, must allow me to carry out a plan of living suitable to my needs by supplying me with the necessary means to do it. And, if you really mean what you say about brotherhood, you will not be hesitant to do so.

In all these years of complete suppression, I have not lived with closed eyes and mind, for I can understand you and your frustrations. And even though you have tried to kill me and my culture, I have allowed you to live unmolested in my backyard with maybe the exception of the years when I fought to protect my expressions of life.

I taught you when you first came to this land to plant certain things in the soil by which to survive. For you did not know the nature of this soil. And even though my methods were not all that productive quantity-wise, they worked. I taught you to take the skins of certain animals and to tan them. When you had learned this, I taught you to sew the hides together, and the protection these methods provided was far better than you employed. In your newness to this country, I took the time to teach you and you repaid me with death. But now, my brothers, don't you think it is only fair and almost past time when you show me your appreciation by allowing me from here on out to live in the way I see fit? Don't you think I should have a choice in the way I want to protect my own country? For once, allow me to decide if I want to go off and to fight in the wars you start and to perish as you obviously relish at the thought of for egotistic reasons. Allow me to live under my own laws as before, and I will not interfere with yours. Allow me to have control over my homelands that are called reservations, and if I want to be neutral where other countries are concerned, let me. Let me walk this land where I was born and where the spirits of my ancestors still sing in my songs. And, allow me to worship as I myself see fit. For have you not said that God is a just God? And if he is, he will not mind. For even though my ways of worship are different than those of yours, they still praise and thank the same thought. And allow me to have a seat in your United Nations. And if I want, let me beat on the table with my shoe while I voice my objections as you have allowed others to do. And if I so desire, let me speak as alternatively as you.

And when you have allowed me all these rights as are the rights of man that you wrote of, then at a point in time, let us meet on a neutral ground. And after we have prayed, thanking the spirits, let us smoke the pipe of man together. And, while we smoke, let us both see how the other is made. And then before the pipe goes out and before our spirits depart, let us take the other by the hand and speak the words, "I love you, my brother, and forever you will remain my brother." And then forever like the blowing wind, and with feelings deeper than the reaches of space and warmer than the radiance of the sun, let us live as brothers in peace.

31 *Leo Tolstoy*

A man caught in the turmoils and social upheavals of his time, Leo Tolstoy was one of the giants of his age. His philosophy was based on a radical understanding of the ethical demands of Christianity. He was an artist, a pioneer in new educational forms, and a theoretician of non-violence. He is a man whose influence is still being felt.

In the first selection,* Tolstoy discusses the states of the Christian world. The second selection ** is the text of a letter addressed to The Daily Chronicle. *The final selection *** is a letter Tolstoy wrote to Ernst Schramm, a young draftee of the Hessian army, in 1899. This was Tolstoy's second letter to Schramm; however, before it reached him, Schramm had left his native land to avoid conscription.*

States of the Christian World

The states of the Christian world have not only reached, but in our day have passed, the limits toward which the states of ancient times were approaching before their dismemberment. We can see this from the fact that each step we make today toward material progress not only does not advance us toward the general well-being, but shows us, on the contrary, that all these technical improvements only increase

* Reprinted from *The Law of Love and the Law of Violence* (New York: Holt, Rinehart and Winston, 1970).

** Reprinted from *On Civil Disobedience and Non-Violence* (New York: Bergman Press, 1967).

*** Reprinted with the permission of the Houghton Library of Harvard University.

our miseries. One can imagine other machines, submarine, subterranean and aerial, for transporting men with the rapidity of lightning; one could multiply to infinity the means of propagating human speech and thought, but it would remain no less the case that these travelers, so comfortably and rapidly transported, are neither willing nor able to commit anything but evil, and the thoughts and words they pour forth would only incite men to further harm. As to the beautifully perfected armaments of destruction, which, while diminishing the risk of those who employ them, make carnage easier, they only give further proof of the impossibility of persevering in the direction we are going.

Thus, the horror of the situation of the Christian world has a double aspect: on the one hand the absence of a moral principle of union, and on the other a gradual lowering of man to a degree below that of the animals, in spite of his intellectual progress and the complexity of the lies that hide from us our misery and our cruelty.

The lies cover the cruelty, the cruelty causes the spreading of the lies, and both increase like insidious snowballs. But everything must come to an end. And I believe that a crisis in this horrible situation is approaching. The evils, resulting from the lack of a religious ideal corresponding to our epoch, are the inevitable conditions of progress; they should as inevitably disappear after the adoption of such an ideal.

Reply to Critics

Since the appearance of my book, "The Kingdom of God Is Within Us," and my articles on "Patriotism and Christianity," I often hear and read in articles and letters addressed to me, arguments against, I will not say the ideas expressed in those books, but against such misconstructions as are put upon them. This is done sometimes consciously, but very often unwittingly, and is wholly due to a want of understanding of the spirit of the Christian religion.

"It is all very well," they say; "despotism, capital punishment, wars, the arming of all Europe, the precarious state of the working-classes, are indeed great evils, and you are right in condemning all this; but how can we do without government? What will you give instead of it? Being ourselves men, with a limited knowledge and intellect, have we the right, just because it seems best to us, to destroy that order of things which has helped our forefathers to attain the present state of civilization and its advantages? If you destroy the State, you must put something in its place. How can we run the risk of all the calamities which might ensue if government was abolished?"

But the fact is that the Christian doctrine, in its true sense, never proposed to abolish anything, nor to change any human organization. The very thing which distinguishes Christian religion from all other religions and social doctrines is that it gives men the possibilities of a real and good life, not by means of general laws regulating the lives of all men, but by enlightening each individual man with regard to the sense of his own life, by showing him wherein consists the evil and the real good of his life. And the sense of life thus imparted to man by the Christian doctrine is so simple, so convincing, and leaves so little room for doubt, that if once man understands it, and, therefore, conceives wherein is the real good and the real evil of his life, he can never again consciously do what he considers to be the evil of his life, nor abstain from doing what he considers to be the real good of it, as surely as a plant cannot help turning toward light, and water cannot help running downward.

The sense of life, as shown by the Christian religion, consists in living so as to do the will of Him who sent us into life, from whom we are come, and to whom we shall return. The evil of our life consists in acting against this will, and the good in fulfilling it. And the rule given to us for the fulfillment of this will is so very plain and simple that it is impossible not to understand, or to misunderstand it.

If you cannot do unto others what you would that they should do to you, at least do not unto them what you would not that they should do unto you.

If you would not be made to work ten hours at a stretch in factories or in mines, if you would not have your children hungry, cold, and ignorant, if you would not be robbed of the land that feeds you, if you would not be shut up in prisons and sent to the gallows or hanged for committing an unlawful deed through passion or ignorance, if you would not suffer wounds nor be killed in war—do not do this to others. All this is so simple and straightforward, and admits of so little doubt, that it is impossible for the simplest child not to understand, nor for the cleverest man to refute it. It is impossible to refute this law, especially because this law is given to us, not only by all the wisest men of the world, not only by the Man who is considered to be God by the majority of Christians, but because it is written in our minds and hearts.

Let us imagine a servant in his lord's power, appointed by his master to a task he loves and understands. If this man were to be addressed by men whom he knows to be dependent on his master in the same way as he is, to whom smaller tasks are set at which they will not work, and who would entreat him for his own good and for the good of other men to do what is directly opposed to his lord's plain commandments, what answer can any reasonable servant give to such entreaties? But this simile is far from fully expressing what a Christian must feel when he is called upon to take an active part in oppressing, robbing people of their land, in executing them, in waging war, and so on, all things which governments call upon us to do; for, however binding the commands of that master may have been to his servant, they can never be compared to that unquestionable knowledge which every man, as long as he is not corrupted by false doctrines, does possess, that he cannot and must not do unto others what he does not wish to be done unto him, and therefore cannot and must not take part in all things opposed to the rule of his Master, which are imposed upon him by governments.

Therefore the question for a Christian does not lie in this: whether or not a man has the right to destroy the existing order of things, and to establish another in its stead, or to decide which kind of government will be the best, as the question is sometimes purposely and very often unintentionally put by the enemies of Christianity (the Christian does not think about the general order of things, but leaves the guidance of them to God, for he firmly believes God has implanted His law in our minds and hearts, that there may be order, not disorder, and that nothing but good can arise from our following the unquestionable law of God, which has been so plainly manifested to us); but the question, the decision of which is not optional, but unavoidable, and which daily presents itself for a Christian to decide, is: How am I to act in the dilemma which is constantly before me? Shall I form part of a government which recognizes the right to own landed property by men who never work on it, which levies taxes on the poor in order to give them to the rich, which condemns erring men to gallows and death, which sends out soldiers to commit murder, which depraves whole races of men by means of opium and brandy, etc., or shall I refuse to take a share in a government, the doings of which are contrary to my conscience? But what will come of it, what sort of State will there be, if I act in this way, is a thing I do not know and which I shall not say I do not wish to know, but which I cannot know.

The main strength of Christ's teaching consists especially in this: that he brought the question of conduct from a world of conjecture and eternal doubt, down to a firm and indisputable ground. Some people say, "But we also do not deny the evils of the existing order and the necessity of changing it, but we wish to change it, not suddenly, by means of refusing to take any part in the government, but, on the contrary, by participating in the government, by gaining more and more freedom, political rights, and obtaining the election of the true friends of the people and the enemies of all violence."

This would be very well, if taking part in one's government and trying to improve it could coincide with the aim of human life. But, unfortunately, it not only does not coincide, but is quite opposed to it.

Supposing human life to be limited to this world, its aim can consist only in man's individual happiness; if, on the other hand, life does not end in this world, its aim can consist only in doing the will of God. In both cases it does not coincide with the progress of governments. If it lies here, in man's personal happiness, and if life ends here, what should I care about the future prosperity of a government which will come about when, in all probability, I shall be there no more? But if my life is immortal, then the prosperity of the English, the Russian, the German, or any other state which is to come in the twentieth century, is too paltry an aim for me, and can never satisfy the cravings of my immortal soul. A sufficient aim for my life is either my immediate personal good, which does not coincide with the government measures and improvements, or the fulfillment of the will of God, which also not only cannot be conciliated with the requirements of government, but is quite opposed to them. The vital question not only for a Christian, but, I think, for any reasonable being, when he is summoned to take part in governmental acts, lies not in the prosperity of his state or government, but in this question:

"Wilt thou, a being of reason and goodness, who comes today and may vanish tomorrow, wilt thou, if thou believest in the existence of God, act against His law and His will, knowing that any moment thou canst return to Him; or, if thou dost not believe in Him, wilt thou, knowing that if thou errest thou shalt never be able to redeem thy error, wilt thou, nevertheless, act in opposition to the principles of reason and love, by which alone thou canst be guided in life? Wilt thou, at the request of thy government, take oaths, defend, by compulsion, the owner of land or capital, wilt thou pay taxes for keeping policemen, soldiers, warships, wilt thou take part in parliaments, law courts, condemnations and wars?"

And to all this—I will not say for a Christian, but for a reasonable being—there can be but one answer: "No, I cannot, and will not." But they say, "This will destroy the State and the existing order." If the fulfillment of the will of God is destroying the existing order, is it not a proof that this existing order is contrary to the will of God, and ought to be destroyed?

Advice to a Draftee

In my last letter I answered your question as well as I could. It is not only Christians but all just people who must refuse to become soldiers—that is, to be ready on another's command (for this is what a soldier's duty actually consists of) to kill all those one is ordered to kill. The question as you state it—which is more useful, to become a good teacher or to suffer for rejecting conscription?—is falsely stated. The question is falsely stated because it is wrong for us to determine our actions according to their results, to view actions merely as useful or destructive. In the choice of our actions we can be led by their advantages or disadvantages only when the actions themselves are not opposed to the demands of morality.

We can stay home, go abroad, or concern ourselves with farming or science according to what we find useful for ourselves or others; for neither in domestic life, foreign travel, farming, nor science is there anything immoral. But under no circumstance can we inflict violence on people, torture or kill them because we think such acts could be of use to us or to others. We cannot and may not do such things, especially because we can never be sure of the results of our actions. Often actions which seem the most advantageous of all turn out in fact to be destructive; and the reverse is also true.

The question should not be stated: which is more useful, to be a good teacher or go to jail for refusing conscription? but rather: what should a man do who has been called upon for military service—that is, called upon to kill or to prepare himself to kill?

And to this question, for a person who understands the true meaning of military service and who wants to be moral, there is only one clear and incontrovertible answer: such a person must refuse to take part in military service no matter what consequences this refusal may have. It may seem to us that this refusal could be futile or even harmful, and that it would be a far more useful thing, after serving one's time, to become a good village teacher. But in the same way, Christ could have judged it more useful for himself to be a good carpenter and submit to all the principles of the Pharisees than to die in obscurity as he did, repudiated and forgotten by everyone.

Moral acts are distinguished from all other acts by the fact that they operate independently of any predictable advantage to ourselves or to others. No matter how dangerous the situation may be of a man who finds himself in the power of robbers who demand that he take part in plundering, murder, and rape, a moral person cannot take part. Is not military service the same thing? Is one not required to agree to the deaths of all those one is commanded to kill?

But how can one refuse to do what everyone does, what everyone finds unavoidable and necessary? Or, must one do what no one does and what everyone considers unnecessary or even stupid and bad? No matter how strange it sounds, this strange argument is the main one offered against those moral acts which in our times face you and every other person called up for military service. But this argument is even more incorrect than the one which would make a moral action dependent upon considerations of advantage.

If I, finding myself in a crowd of running people, run with the crowd without knowing where, it is obvious that I have given myself up to mass hysteria; but if by chance I should push my way to the front, or be gifted with sharper sight than the others, or receive information that this crowd was racing to attack human beings and toward its own corruption, would I really not stop and tell the people what might rescue them? Would I go on running and do these things which I knew to be bad or corrupt? This is the situation of every individual called up for military service, if he knows what military service means.

I can well understand that you, a young man full of life, loving and loved by your mother, friends, perhaps a young woman, think with a natural terror about what awaits you if you refuse conscription; and perhaps you will not feel strong enough to bear the consequences of refusal, and knowing your weakness, will submit and become a soldier. I understand completely, and I do not for a moment allow myself to blame you, knowing very well that in your place I might perhaps do the same thing. Only do not say that you did it because it was useful or because everyone does it. If you did it, know that you did wrong.

In every person's life there are moments in which he can know himself, tell himself who he is, whether he is a man who values his human dignity above his life or a weak creature who does not know his dignity and is concerned merely with being useful (chiefly to himself). This is the situation of a man who goes out to defend his honor in a duel or a soldier who goes into battle (although here the concepts of life are wrong). It is the situation of a doctor or a priest called to someone sick with plague, of a man in a burning house or a sinking ship who must decide whether to let the weaker go first or shove them aside and save himself. It is the situation of a man in poverty who accepts or rejects a bribe. And in our times, it is the situation of a man called to military service. For a man who knows its significance, the call to the army is perhaps the only opportunity for him to behave as a morally free creature and fulfill the highest requirement of his life—or else merely to keep his advantage in sight like an animal and thus remain slavishly submissive and servile until humanity becomes degraded and stupid.

For these reasons I answered your question whether one has to refuse to do military service with a categorical "yes"—if you understand the meaning of military service (and if you did not understand it then, you do now) and if you want to behave as a moral person living in our times must.

Please excuse me if these words are harsh. The subject is so important that one cannot be careful enough in expressing oneself so as to avoid false interpretation.

Leo Tolstoy

RELATED READING BY LEO TOLSTOY

The Kingdom of God Is Within You (New York: Farrar, Straus & Giroux, 1905).

32 Mark Twain

One of America's most noted humorists, Mark Twain also spoke with an eloquent voice against the ravages of war. The poem reproduced here* was published posthumously because, as he bitterly observed: "I have told the whole truth . . . and only dead men can tell the truth in this world." His insight and understanding of human nature is timeless and telling.

The War Prayer

It was a time of great and
exalting excitement.

The country was up in arms,
the war was on,
in every breast
burned the holy fire of patriotism;
the drums were beating,
the bands playing,
the toy pistols popping,
the bunched firecrackers
hissing and spluttering;
on every hand and far down
the receding and fading spread
of roofs and balconies
a fluttering wilderness of flags
flashed in the sun;
daily the young volunteers marched
down the wide avenue
gay and fine in their new uniforms,

* Reprinted from *Europe and Elsewhere* by Mark Twain. Copyright 1923 by The Mark Twain Company; renewed 1951 by The Mark Twain Company. Reprinted by permission of Harper & Row, Publishers, Inc.

the proud fathers and mothers
and sisters and sweethearts
cheering them with voices
choked with happy emotion
as they swung by;
nightly the packed mass meetings
listened, panting, to patriot oratory
which stirred the deepest deeps
of their hearts
and which they interrupted
at briefest intervals
with cyclones of applause,
the tears running down their cheeks
the while;
in the churches the pastors preached
devotion to flag and country
and invoked the God of Battles,
beseeching His aid in our good cause
in outpouring of fervid eloquence
which moved every listener.
It was indeed a glad and gracious time,
and the half-dozen rash spirits
that ventured to disapprove of the war
and cast a doubt upon its righteousness
straightway got such a stern
and angry warning
that for their personal safety's sake
they quickly shrank out of sight
and offended no more in that way.

Sunday morning came—
next day the battalions would leave
for the front;
the church was filled;
the volunteers were there,
their young faces
alight with martial dreams—
visions of the stern advance,
the gathering momentum,

the rushing charge, the flashing sabers,
the flight of the foe, the tumult,
the enveloping smoke, the fierce pursuit,
the surrender!—
then home from the war,
bronzed heroes, welcomed, adored,
submerged in golden seas of glory!
With the volunteers sat their dear ones,
proud, happy, and envied
by the neighbors and friends
who had no sons and brothers
to send forth to the field of honor,
there to win for the flag or failing,
die the noblest of noble deaths.
The service proceeded; a war chapter
from the Old Testament was read;
the first prayer was said;
it was followed by an organ burst
that shook the building,
and with one impulse the house rose,
with glowing eyes and beating hearts,
and poured out
that tremendous invocation—

> *God the all-terrible!*
> *Thou who ordainest,*
> *Thunder thy clarion*
> *and lightning thy sword!*

Then came the "long" prayer.
None could remember the like of it
for passionate pleading
and moving and beautiful language.
The burden of its supplication was
that an ever-merciful and benignant
Father of us all would watch over
our noble young soldiers
and aid, comfort, and encourage them
in their patriotic work;
bless them, shield them in the day

of battle and the hour of peril,
bear them in His mighty hand,
make them strong and confident,
invincible in the bloody onset;
help them to crush the foe,
grant to them
and to their flag and country
imperishable honor and glory—

An aged stranger entered and moved
with slow and noiseless step
up the main aisle,
his eyes fixed upon the minister,
his long body clothed in a robe
that reached to his feet, his head bare,
his white hair descending
in a frothy cataract to his shoulders,
his seamy face unnaturally pale,
pale even to ghastliness.
With all eyes following him
and wondering,
he made his silent way;
without pausing, he ascended
to the preacher's side
and stood there, waiting.
With shut lids the preacher,
unconscious of his presence,
continued his moving prayer,
and at last finished it with the words,
uttered in fervent appeal,
"Bless our arms,
grant us the victory,
O Lord our God,
Father and Protector
of our land and flag!"

The stranger touched his arm,
motioned him to step aside—
which the startled minister did—
and took his place.

During some moments
he surveyed the spellbound audience
with solemn eyes in which burned
an uncanny light;
then in a deep voice he said:

"I come from the Throne—
bearing a message from Almighty God!"
The words smote the house with a shock;
if the stranger perceived it
he gave no attention.
"He has heard the prayer
of His servant your shepherd
and will grant it
if such shall be your desire
after I, His messenger,
shall have explained to you its import—
that is to say, its full import.
For it is like unto
many of the prayers of men,
in that it asks for more
than he who utters it is aware of—
except he pause and think.

"God's servant and yours
has prayed his prayer.
Has he paused and taken thought?
Is it one prayer?
No, it is two—
one uttered, the other not.
Both have reached the ear
of Him Who heareth all supplications,
the spoken and the unspoken.
Ponder this—keep it in mind.
If you would beseech
a blessing upon yourself, beware!
lest without intent
you invoke a curse upon a neighbor
at the same time.
If you pray for the blessing of rain

upon your crop which needs it,
by that act you are possibly praying
for a curse upon some neighbor's crop
which may not need rain
and can be injured by it.

"You have heard your servant's prayer—
the uttered part of it.
I am commissioned of God
to put into words the other part of it—
that part which the pastor,
and also you in your hearts,
fervently prayed silently.
And ignorantly and unthinkingly?
God grant that it was so!
You heard these words:
'Grant us the victory,
O Lord our God!'
That is sufficient.
The *whole* of the uttered prayer
is compact into those pregnant words.
Elaborations were not necessary.
When you have prayed for victory
you have prayed for
many unmentioned results
which follow victory—*must* follow it,
cannot help but follow it.
Upon the listening spirit
of God the Father fell also
the unspoken part of the prayer.
He commandeth me
to put it into words.

LISTEN!

"O Lord our Father,

our young patriots,
idols of our hearts,

go forth to battle—
be Thou near them!
With them, in spirit,
    we also go forth
from the sweet peace
of our beloved firesides
    to smite the foe.

O Lord our God,

    help us
to tear their soldiers
    to bloody shreds
        with our shells;

    help us
to cover their smiling fields
    with the pale forms
    of their patriot dead;

    help us
to drown the thunder
    of the guns
    with the shrieks
    of their wounded,
    writhing in pain;

    help us
to lay waste
their humble homes
with a hurricane of fire;

    help us
to wring the hearts
of their unoffending widows
    with unavailing grief;

    help us
to turn them out roofless

with their little children
to wander unfriended
    the wastes
of their desolated land

    in rags and hunger
    and thirst,
sports of the sun flames
    of summer
and the icy winds
    of winter,

broken in spirit,

worn with travail,

    imploring Thee
for the refuge of the grave
    and denied it—

    for our sakes
who adore Thee, Lord,

blast their hopes,

blight their lives,

protract their bitter pilgrimage,

make heavy their steps,

water their way with their tears,

    stain the white snow
    with the blood
of their wounded feet!

    We ask it,
    in the spirit of love,
of Him Who is the Source of Love,

and Who is the ever-faithful
          refuge and friend
of all that are sore beset

          and seek His aid
with humble and contrite hearts.

AMEN.

After a pause:

"Ye have prayed it;
if ye still desire it,
speak!
The messenger of the
Most High waits."

It was believed afterward
that the man was a lunatic,
because there was no sense
in what he said.

RELATED READING BY MARK TWAIN

Portable Mark Twain, Bernard de Voto, ed. (New York: Viking Press,
     1946).

33 Simone Weil

A French writer, and part of the French Resistance to the Nazi regime, Simone Weil was 24 when she wrote this article, "Reflections on War." She was born a Jew, but rejected Judaism and became sympathetic to the Catholic Church. Thomas Merton has said of her, "Simone Weil is one of those brilliant and independent French thinkers who were able to articulate the deepest concerns of Europe in the first half of this century."

Reflections on War

Revolutionary war is the grave of revolution. And it will be that as long as the soldiers themselves, or rather the armed citizenry, are not given the means of waging war without a directing apparatus, without police pressure, without court-martial, without punishment for deserters. Once in modern history was a war carried on in this manner—under the Commune. Everybody knows with what results. It seems that revolution engaged in war has only the choice of either succumbing under the murderous blows of counterrevolution or transforming itself into counterrevolution through the very mechanism of the military struggle.

The perspectives of a revolution seem therefore quite restricted. For can a revolution avoid war? It is, however, on this feeble chance that we must stake everything or abandon all hope. An advanced country will not encounter, in case of revolution, the difficulties which in backward Russia served as a base for the barbarous regime of Stalin. But a war of any scope will give rise to others as formidable.

For mighty reasons a war undertaken by a bourgeois state cannot but transform power into despotism and subjection into assas-

171

sination. If war sometimes appears as a revolutionary factor, it is only in the sense that it constitutes an incomparable test for the functioning of the state. In contact with war, a badly organized apparatus collapses. But if the war does not end soon, or if it starts up again, or if the decomposition of the state has not gone far enough, the situation results in revolutions, which, according to Marx's formula, perfect the state apparatus instead of shattering it. That is what has always happened up to now.

In our time the difficulty developed by war to a high degree is especially that resulting from the ever growing opposition between the state apparatus and the capitalist system. The Briey affair during the last war provides us with a striking example. The last war brought to several state apparatuses a certain authority over economic matters. (This gave rise to the quite erroneous term of "war socialism.") Later the capitalist system returned to an almost normal manner of functioning, in spite of custom barriers, quotas and national monetary systems. There is no doubt that in the next war things will go a little farther. We know that quantity can transform itself into quality. In this sense, war can constitute a revolutionary factor in our time, but only if one wants to give the term "revolution" the meaning given to it by the Nazis. Like economic depression, a war will arouse hatred against capitalists, and this hatred, exploited for "national unity," will benefit the state apparatus and not the workers. Furthermore, to realize the kinship of war and fascism, one has but to recall those fascist tracts appealing to "the soldierly spirit" and "front-line socialism." In war, as in fascism, the essential "point" is the obliteration of the individual by a state bureaucracy serving a rabid fanaticism. Whatever the demagogues may say, the damage the capitalist system suffers at the hands of either of these phenomena can only still further weaken all human values.

The absurdity of an antifascist struggle which chooses war as its means of action thus appears quite clear. Not only would this mean to fight barbarous oppression by crushing peoples under the weight of an even more barbarous massacre. It would actually mean spreading under another form the very regime that we want to suppress. It is childish to suppose that a state apparatus rendered powerful by a victorious war would lighten the oppression exercised over its own people by the enemy state apparatus. It is even more childish to suppose that the victorious state apparatus would permit a proletarian revolution to break out in the defeated country without drowning it immediately in blood. As for bourgeois democracy being annihilated by fascism, a war would not do away with this threat but would reinforce and extend the causes that now render it possible.

It seems that, generally speaking, history is more and more forcing every political actor to choose between aggravating the oppression exercised by the various state apparatuses and carrying on a merciless struggle against these apparatuses in order to shatter them. Indeed, the almost insoluble difficulties presenting themselves nowadays almost justify the pure and simple abandonment of the struggle. But if we are not to renounce all action, we must understand that we can struggle against the state apparatus only inside the country. And notably in case of war, we must choose between hindering the functioning of the military machine of which we are ourselves so many cogs and blindly aiding that machine to continue to crush human lives.

Thus Karl Liebknecht's famous words, "The main enemy is at home," take on their full significance and are revealed to be applicable to all wars in which soldiers are reduced to the condition of passive matter in the hands of a bureaucratic and military apparatus. This means that as long as the present war technique continues, these words apply to any war, absolutely speaking. And in our time we cannot foresee the advent of another technique. In production as in war, the increasingly collective manner with which forces are operated has not modified the essentially individual functions of decision and management. It has only placed more and more of the hands and lives of the mass at the disposal of the commanding apparatuses.

Until we discover how to avoid, in the very act of production or of fighting, the domination of an apparatus over the mass, so long will every revolutionary attempt have in it something of the hopeless. For if we do know what system of production and combat we aspire with all our heart to destroy, we do not know what acceptable system could replace it. Furthermore, every attempt at reform appears puerile in face of the blind necessities implied in the operation of the monstrous social machine. Our society resembles an immense machine that ceaselessly snatches and devours human beings and which no one knows how to master. And they who sacrifice themselves for social progress are like persons who try to catch hold of the wheels and the transmission belts in order to stop the machine and are destroyed in their attempts.

But the impotence one feels today—an impotence we should never consider permanent—does not excuse one from remaining true to oneself, nor does it excuse capitulation to the enemy, whatever mask he may wear. Whether the mask is labeled fascism, democracy, or dictatorship of the proletariat, our great adversary remains The Apparatus—the bureaucracy, the police, the military. Not the one facing us across the frontier or the battle lines, which is not so much our enemy as our brothers' enemy, but the one that calls itself our protector and makes us its slaves. No matter what the circumstances, the worst betrayal will always be to subordinate ourselves to this Apparatus, and to trample underfoot, in its service, all human values in ourselves and in others.

OTHER WORKS BY SIMONE WEIL

On Science, Necessity, and the Love of God, Richard Rees, ed. (London: Oxford University Press, 1968).
Waiting for God (New York: Capricorn Books, 1959).
The Need for Roots (New York: Putnam Books, 1952).